The
CHURCH
SECRETARY'S
HANDBOOK

*Patricia
McKenna
Seraydarian*

Tyndale House
Publishers, Inc.
Wheaton, Illinois

To the men in my life —

James M. Seraydarian, *my husband*

David L. McKenna, *my brother*

L. Edward Davis, *my pastor*

First printing, May 1982
Library of Congress Catalog Card Number 81-85151
ISBN 0-8423-0281-6
Copyright © 1982 by Patricia McKenna Seraydarian
Printed in the United States of America

CONTENTS

Part One

THE PEOPLE

1
AN EXTENSION
OF THE TYPEWRITER
OR A PLACE
IN THE KINGDOM?

God has given each of you special abilities . . . 1 Peter
4:10, TLB

*And whatever you do or say, let it be as a representative
of the Lord Jesus* . . . Col. 3:17, TLB

The office telephone is ringing again, just as it has all morning. Your fingers are racing over the typewriter keys as
you prepare sermon copy for a one o'clock printer's deadline. You quickly reach for the phone. On the other end is a
bright, cheery voice bubbling, "Oh, is this the church secretary? I'm Terri New Member, and I'm so happy to talk
with you. I just know you can answer all my questions."
And, seemingly without pausing for breath, she proceeds
to ask numerous questions, none of which is urgent—at
least from your perspective.

Whoosh! Now you know how a balloon feels when it is
punctured. Upon hanging up the receiver, you glance at
the clock and realize that only by working through lunch
hour *again* can you meet the deadline.

A typical morning in the life of the church secretary?
Yes! If it hadn't been talkative Terri, it would probably
have been Demanding Dan, Lonely Lillian, Chairman

Charles, Syrupy Sylvia, or some other equally disturbing soul within the congregation.

You sometimes think to yourself, "Don't those people realize I have a job to do? Don't they know I have deadlines? Why do they all think I can talk with them at any time, at any length?"

There you are—right in the middle of one of those situations that has come to be known as "bad news—good news." The "bad news" is that you return to your typing with very mixed feelings of anxiety, frustration, tension, and perhaps even anger. But the "good news" is that the situation need not evoke any of those feelings. And the "better news" is that, if such feelings do emerge, you can cope with them because *you* control them; they don't control you!

Now, if you are like me, you are skeptical of anyone who dares to suggest that she has *the* answer to your problem. I admit I may not have *the* answer, but I have *an* answer. And that answer is you!

"Why me?" you ask.

Think about the elements of your job: the job itself, the church members, the pastor, and yourself. The job is not likely to change, and the members are even less likely to change, especially since they don't even know they are a problem. Gone are the days when the pastor moved every three years. That leaves one possible area of adjustment that you can control—yourself!

Of course, there are specific suggestions to be made for possible changes in your job from an efficiency standpoint, and these will be included in later chapters. However, as desirable as such measures are, their successful implementation depends on people, and again, that brings us back to you. You are the key element in effecting change!

Whether or not you use that key to unlock the door to greater job satisfaction is dependent upon your understanding of two critical factors: (1) your career concept, and (2) your commitment. You are the only person who can explore and ultimately assess the role these two factors play in your job and your life.

Self-assessment is always a difficult process. First of all, we are not conditioned to or comfortable with admitting the strengths of our own personalities. In fact, "self-image" appears to be at an all-time low for many of us. Evidence of this is seen in the unprecedented numbers of people flocking to attend human potential seminars, TM sessions, behavior modification groups, yoga classes, etc.

Second, it is always easier to spot the faults in someone else. "Why is she like that?" is a much-asked question.

In addition, both of the factors mentioned are highly personal and thus the candidness of your judgment might be affected. As you explore these areas in yourself, try not to begin with any preconceived notions, either positive or negative. Be equally ready to say, "I like this about me," or "I don't like that about myself."

Remember, your self-assessment is only a starting point. Your goal is to strengthen good points, modify less desirable ones, or change radically those that appear to be out of place in a Christian's life.

YOUR CAREER CONCEPT

What is a career? What is a job? Is there a difference between the two? If so, how does the difference affect you?

First, talking about careers, in the strictest sense of that word, is a very popular subject these days. A great deal of time, effort, and monies is being expended by public agencies at all levels to help youngsters better prepare themselves for making career choices. Such a movement is probably long overdue, especially for females. For example, girls are now being encouraged to think in terms of "doctor" as well as "nurse," "administrator" as well as "teacher," and "manager" as well as "secretary."

Second, uniquely to the Christian, "career" and "vocation" may be used interchangeably. Each of us has a vocation—the doctor, the minister, the housewife. God calls us first to salvation and second to vocation. Recognizing that each of us has a unique job to perform within the body of Christ gives "career" a whole new dimension.

Many of you did not have such a luxury of choice for a career as is mentioned earlier. How well I recall the total approval of my parents when I elected shorthand and typing as a high school student. Those were skills I could fall back on when I married and had children—marriage and a family being an assumption. While achieving a college education was neither discouraged nor encouraged, becoming a secretary was a highly desirable goal. It was a career to which one aspired. The image was good.

Something has happened—that image has become tarnished. Being a secretary is too often merely a job rather than a career. What then is the distinction between the two?

Looking at the definition of the two terms may help. Webster's dictionary defines a career as "a profession for which one trains and which is undertaken as a permanent calling," whereas a job is defined as a "specific duty, role, or function."

Think of your own work experiences. Do you recall being employed in a job as a means to an end? Perhaps you were a baby-sitter earning spending money as a teenager. Maybe you worked as a waitress to support your education. Or you might have done any variety of odd jobs in order to buy a car. Regardless of what form such work took, remember how temporary you considered such employment? In a sense, you were putting in your time in order to fulfill an immediate need. Those were jobs! Granted, in some cases, those "jobs" permitted you to launch a "career."

Then, do you recall your first job as a secretary? Even though that position may pale in comparison to others you have held since, do you remember having a feeling of accomplishment? It was a very important beginning. You saw the job as having a purpose—giving you needed experience to obtain a better position or to assume more responsibility. That's career thinking—seeing a job as part of a long-range goal.

That is the critical factor in a career—long-range thinking, probably covering a major portion of your life. Within that career may be one or several jobs, part-time or full-time.

When you can conceptualize that relationship, you are ready to consider the next question: Does the difference affect me?

If, in fact, you decide that you have a job rather than a career, then the answer may be "No." However, if like a growing number of women, you have a career, then the answer is definitely "Yes."

How, then, does it affect you? First, knowing the difference may have a direct bearing on personal and professional growth. A recent book[1] studied the relationship between job and career, attempting to determine why so few women occupy managerial positions. After both men and women were interviewed, the study concluded that they each define "job" and "career" differently. Specifically, the women had difficulty relating the one to the other or seeing the job as a part of the career whole. More importantly, the inability to form that relationship within one's mind was cited as a major factor in the small percentage of women in managerial positions.

If women, in general, have difficulty establishing that relationship, how much more difficult it can be for Christian women. Many of them are reluctant to even think in career terms because they are dealing with a degree of guilt brought on by well-meaning leaders who pull them in various directions, suggesting that the sole obligation of women is to their homes and families. The implication is strong in Christian circles that a successful blending of career and family is impossible. I have to ask, Why? Why

[1]Margaret and Anne Jardin Hennig, *The Managerial Woman* (Garden City, NY: Anchor Press/Doubleday, 1977).

should that be the exclusive right of non-Christians?

Combining a career and a family is never an easy task; however, "difficult" and "impossible" are not synonymous. Whether you have a job or a career may be insignificant from a Christian standpoint, but whether you have your priorities straight is very significant. Priorities are what it's all about! If you are a career woman and enjoy being one, say so! If you are a wife and mother and enjoy being one, say so! And if you are successfully combining all those roles, say so! One of our problems as Christians is that we are so aware of what we're supposed to be that we're afraid to admit to what we are.

Second, the small percentage of women in managerial positions may not seem too important to you. As a part-time secretary or as a secretary in a small church, you may think that the chance of moving into a managerial position is nonexistent. Perhaps you are thinking in terms of titles rather than responsibilities, and that brings our discussion to another point—your perspective.

We all like titles—the more important they sound, the better. However, the facts are that the pressure being exerted by society to promote women has resulted in many very capable people being given a new title with little or no change in their jobs. As a result, there are many administrative assistants in offices today who are performing the same tasks they have always performed, drawing essentially the same salary, but carrying a new title. One executive secretary, recently retitled administrative assistant, remarked to me, "I'm not an administrative assistant; I'm still a secretary. My job has not changed." She would gladly have traded the emptiness of the new title for the fulfillment of added responsibilities.

Let's forget the glamour of titles for the moment and talk about career growth within the context of your job. How do your tasks differ from what they were when you were first employed? What new responsibilities have been given to you? How has your decision-making changed? Do

14

you feel that you manage your office, or do the office and people in it manage you? If you are truly on a career path, you should be able to cite specific areas of growth.

For too many secretaries such a sense of growth is not clear or is even nonexistent. If you are in that group, consider these questions as a starting point:

Do you always rely on your pastor for direction, or are you a self-starter? Have you reorganized your work area lately, or are you using the same methods and procedures you always have? Can others rely on you to follow through, or do you frequently need reminders? When was the last time you took a refresher course, visited an equipment demonstration, or attended a professional meeting related to your job? Look around your office; perhaps you can add to this list.

Remember, if you wait for the pastor to make you a manager, you may have a long wait. But you can promote yourself—by attitude, by efficiency, by reliability. You can grow careerwise, without ever leaving your present job.

A third factor to be considered in this discussion of your career is your specific occupation—church secretary. For example, why aren't you a nurse, a teacher, or a salesperson? Are you a church secretary by choice or by chance? Perhaps you chose to become a secretary and by chance your job happens to be in a church. Then, let me ask, if you had a choice of occupations today, would your decision be the same? Or are you there because you want to be?

As we all know, choosing a specific occupation can cause some very anxious moments for young people, particularly for Christian young people. During the years I attended a Christian college, I recall encountering numerous very confused, albeit sincere, persons wandering aimlessly through their lives and their studies waiting for God to tell them what to do. How sad! God doesn't need more indecisive people serving him full time! I'm convinced he can only handle them on a part-time basis.

Were you aware that, as a church secretary, you are

uniquely privileged? Christians in secular occupations do not have your opportunity to participate so directly in furthering the cause of Christ and his church. Of necessity a major part of their lives is devoted to promoting the goals of the business or institution where they are employed. They have no lesser sense of vocation than you do regarding their work, but they have fewer opportunities to demonstrate that sensitivity. Their Christian commitment must often be quietly proven by the practice of such principles as diligence, integrity, and a genuine sense of caring. Hopefully, the consistency of those practices will provide other opportunities for them to share the richness of their faith.

This need not be the case with you. In a sense, you are doubly blessed as you have the opportunity to use those skills you have developed for career purposes in a practical application of your commitment.

YOU AND YOUR COMMITMENT

The key to developing that sense of mission is your personal commitment. Without that, you are merely living on the edge of life's greatest adventure. As church secretary, your commitment has three facets: (1) to Jesus Christ; (2) to people; and (3) to professionalism.

Let us look briefly at each of these.

To Jesus Christ. A current classified ad in my local paper reads:

> Personable woman wanted for position of church secretary. Must be an active Christian.

I would like to meet the pastor who is running that ad; it seems as if he has his priorities straight.

First, every employer places a high premium on loyalty. This is no less true of the local pastor. How can he better guarantee loyalty to himself and his church than by hiring a secretary who has first given her loyalty to Jesus Christ?

Second, I do not think that a person other than a committed Christian can be an effective church secretary. Anyone properly trained can type, file, keep books, or manage an office, but only a person with this added dimension can bring to the job the necessary spirit and understanding.

To people. While entering a place of business one day, I noticed a sign hanging over the door that read: "The world's most important people pass through this door." How true that is also of the church, and how aware of that fact the committed secretary is.

The church secretary must show a genuine concern for people (even kids and dogs can spot a phony!). The two minutes she spends on the telephone with a member who needs attention may be far more valuable than the two sentences she might have typed during that time.

I once knew an executive secretary who always took time to greet and chat briefly with anyone who came into her office. Her job was very demanding; the pressures were intense. Yet the person entering her office was never the victim of that pressure.

Have you ever thought, "If I am the only contact a person has with Christ and the church, what is that person's impression?"

Who should have a greater "people sense" than the Christian secretary? We may need to recall that Jesus left us only two commands: To love our God and to love our neighbor. That is quite an assignment. Maybe he knew we couldn't handle more.

To professionalism. Persons in all occupations feel the need to improve or upgrade their professional knowledge from time to time. This should certainly be equally true of the church secretary.

17

That growth may occur in several ways, some of which were mentioned earlier. For example, taking time to become acquainted with the latest equipment and procedures that may contribute to the overall efficiency of your office should be a part of your professional commitment. Or, if your level of efficiency is adversely affected by the level of your skills, you should take the necessary steps to improve them. This may involve pursuing additional education, or it may be simply developing a planned program of self-improvement.

Participation in professional groups and workshops should be a part of the church secretary's life whenever possible. The exchange of ideas that frequently occurs in such settings can be an invaluable aid to your office processes.

Whatever form the professional aspect of your commitment needs to assume, get with it!

AN EXTENSION OF THE TYPEWRITER OR . . .

You have now looked at your career, and you have looked at your commitment. Are you an extension of the typewriter, or do you indeed have a place in the kingdom of God?

Only you can answer that question. Outside observers can only give surface perceptions. The true answer lies within yourself.

Only you can change that answer if it is other than you want it to be. Whether a different job or a new commitment or both are needed, the response must come from you.

In summary, feel professional and act professional; feel committed and act committed.

2
THE BUFFER ZONE

. . . each part in its own special way helps the other parts, so that the whole body is healthy and growing and full of love Eph. 4:16, TLB

If it were possible for me to ask you to define "pastor," I would get a variety of highly personal responses because each of you would be working from the mental image of your own pastor. However, for the church secretary to fully comprehend the meaning of the word, she must look at it from a much broader perspective.

First, in the biblical sense, the pastor is a gifted individual (see Eph. 4:11). Second, in a legal sense, he[1] is a person authorized to perform the rites of a given religion. And, perhaps most important, somewhere in between those two definitions is an individual who fits a wide range of sizes, shapes, and dispositions.

Unlike persons in other occupations who have the luxury of specializing in a single area of job performance, the pastor must truly be all things to all people—preacher, spouse, teacher, parent, counselor, administrator, financial

[1]My apologies for the use of "he" for pastor and "she" for secretary throughout this book. This style is followed simply in the interest of readability.

19

wizard, to name only a few. Furthermore, the inability to perform equally well in each of these areas can make him the easy target of criticism.

And yet, if we move along in the Scriptures to Ephesians 4:12, we find that, while he is gifted as an overseer, he is still only one part of the body of Christ. The ability of that body to function is dependent upon the functions of each of the members. Thus, we may imply that the human resources within a congregation are critical elements in its successful operation, and the secretary who understands the total picture is the one who can truly function as "the buffer zone."

With this broader perspective in mind, there are two key items that determine the effectiveness of the church secretary in relation to the pastor:

(1) The relationships: professional and personal.
(2) The roles: professional and personal.

Let us consider each of these in greater detail.

THE RELATIONSHIPS

The relationship of any employer-employee is two-sided: professional and personal. This is no less true in the pastor-secretary relationship and, in fact, carries some unique responsibilities.

First, the professional relationship. You are both professionals even though you serve in totally different capacities. It may seem harsh to say that the church secretary who accepts her job primarily as a way to serve her Lord may not be prepared for the realities of the job, and that idea is in no way contradictory to the commitment discussion of the first chapter. Let me explain.

The pastor's major role is to oversee the flock; he needs someone to complement his efforts, not take over his role. He needs someone to do the typing and filing, to manage the office, to screen the telephone calls, or, in other words, to do the "nitty-gritty." Your professional worth grows as you are able to free him from details and allow him to pastor. Your sense of serving the Lord may be tested as you clean mimeo ink from your new skirt! Then, realistically, chances are that the pastor has had very little, if any, formal training in organization, planning, or even written communications. He needs you and the unique training you bring to your job. Ultimately, he should be completely worry-free, as far as the day-to-day operation of the church office goes. This can only evolve as you both assume your individual professional roles.

Second, the personal relationship. Some churches select their secretaries from outside their own membership in order to minimize the possibility of personal relationships existing at the outset. Much can be said for that approach, but it is not often the case.

The relationship of the pastor and secretary is a delicate one. As with doctors, lawyers, psychiatrists, and other "people helpers," the possibility of developing a personal dependency is omnipresent. These people tend to be good listeners. Or, as one church secretary described her pastor to me, "He's a good father image." How then do you develop and maintain a healthy personal relationship?

First, a key suggestion—do not use your pastor-employer as your counselor. The close proximity of boss and secretary is often enough to handle. Do not add the dimension of shared confidences of a very personal nature to this relationship.

Second, some additional guidelines:

1. Keep the conversation in all one-to-one conferences strictly on business.
2. Avoid one-on-one lunches and coffee breaks.
3. Don't permit yourself to fantasize—he's not perfect! In fact, he probably even snores!
4. Maintain a healthy, open relationship with his wife.
5. Look and act professional at all times—more on this in the next section.

What if—

To the best of your knowledge, you have done nothing to encourage an unhealthy personal relationship and yet the pastor clearly makes a personal overture? What should you do? Call for the elders of the church? No! It is time for some prayerful soul-searching.

Your first concern should be your own response to the action. How did you feel? Were you pleasantly surprised, or were you repulsed? Either reaction requires immediate action.

Let's assume for a moment that you enjoyed it. Then, there is probably only one way to respond—get out! And the sooner the better. The possibility of defusing the tiniest of sparks originating from two sources is very slim.

But if you were unpleasantly surprised and are clearly at the dilemma stage, then you must handle the situation differently. First, prayerfully ask for courage and guidance and confront him. Talk it out immediately. Declare your disinterest. Remind him of the implications of such actions. But don't forget—he is human; he does make mistakes. Make it very clear that you are disappointed but offer to prayerfully forgive and forget. Suggest that he do the same. In many instances, you may well spare a soul, a family, a congregation, and even a community from the blackest blot that can fall on the Christian church.

THE ROLE

Similar to the question of the relationship, the role of the secretary in the pastoral office has two sides: professional and personal.

Your primary role as a professional is to free the pastor from office details. In fact, "reverse dependency" (the pastor's dependency on you) should evolve as a result of your working together. He should literally be able to drop something on your desk and walk away from it, totally confident that whatever action is needed will be taken—

and on time! How do you build that kind of confidence?

First, it is not a Topsy—it does not just grow. Only as the pastor observes your ability to handle details will he place an increasing amount of confidence in you. However, you can promote this level of confidence by cultivating two traits.

The first of these is *anticipation*. Let's follow through a typical example: The pastor informs you that a church official will be visiting the church for two days. Immediately the gears of your mind should shift into action. Several pertinent questions should be asked: "Do you have a tentative schedule?" "Where will he be staying?" "How will his meals be provided?" "Does he want to meet with anyone other than yourself?" "What can I do to help you prepare for his visit?" This is anticipatory thinking.

But, you say, my pastor has always handled those details. That may be the case, but it may be because no one has ever volunteered to assist. And what if the pastor's response is, "No, thanks. I'll handle the details." Then are you to forget the visit? Absolutely not! This is one of the many instances in which "secretarial subtlety" takes over. (Those of you who are wives understand this completely!) You may convey the impression that you are leaving it alone, but in reality you will make a note of the dates on the calendar. Possibly you will free the calendar of any conflicting appointments except those of the most critical nature. You certainly will arrive early on the day of the visit, prepare a fresh pot of coffee, arrange to have regular cups rather than the ubiquitous styrofoam, and quietly keep anyone else from interrupting during the early part of the meeting. Your efforts will not be unnoticed or unappreciated.

Anticipatory thinking separates the superior secretaries from the mediocre ones. There are two common shortcomings that church secretaries are apt to have. The first of these is the assumption that the pastor does not want help because he does not ask for it. How wrong this one can be. Do you recall the popular television commercial regarding a husband's choice between potatoes and a well-known brand of stuffing mix? Maybe your pastor would also prefer stuffing, if given the choice. The second is the notion that it is not necessary to think on your job. Typing is a mechanical skill; thinking while typing is an art. And to be able to think ahead is a rare treasure. Don't expect the pastor to lay out each step for you. Be two steps ahead of him.

The second step in promoting confidence is *organization*. Some secretaries' desks remind me of the popular wall plaque: "Hard work never bothers me. I can sit and look at it for hours." Specifically, how do you organize?

If your pastor arrives at nine a.m. sharp, ready and eager to work, you should arrive at ten minutes before nine, organize your day's work, review the day's schedule, and greet him totally relaxed, as though you have been there for hours. However, if your pastor is one of those 8:30 birds and you really don't want to get into an early alarm clock contest with him, you must learn to "steal" the last ten or fifteen minutes of the previous day and organize for the next day. Organize and choose priorities.

Some of you are saying, "If she knew my office and my pastor, she would know that I can never organize. There are too many interruptions, too many people who think their jobs are the most important, too many people wanting to talk, and on and on." And I would still reply, "Too little organization."

First, organization is a very personal thing, and any plan must be adapted to meet the needs of your own office. However, you can begin by keeping a log of tasks for one week. A sample log, based on the most frequently performed tasks of church secretaries surveyed for this book, is provided on page 154 of Part II. If you use this log, you will need only to record the frequency of each task.

If you prefer to design your own log, simply write down every task as you do it. If possible, indicate how long it

24

takes to complete the job. Tally the number of phone calls you handle. Jot down the number of visitors to the office. Your log does not need to be a formal listing—just a quick note of each activity in your own brand of shorthand will give you a working list.

At the end of the week, analyze your log. First, check those items that are done on a regular basis—each day, each week, each month. For example, typing the bulletin is done each week; typing the minutes of the church's governing body is more likely a monthly task. Are such jobs done on regularly scheduled days? If not, why not? Because Charlie Chairman never has his items in on time, right? Announce to your world that beginning next week the bulletin will be typed on a certain morning, and then do it! When Charlie Chairman calls you at noon with his urgent message, "secretarial sweetness" comes into play. Apologize profusely, but tell him that the bulletin is already done. After you have perfected this act of "I'm so sorry," Charlie will either shape up or apologize for asking.

Be prepared to take some criticism for assuming a hard line. Just smile and remember that you are the one responsible for producing the bulletin and not the critics. Shortly after I became secretary of the Board of Deacons for my church, I was labeled "General Seraydarian." I just smiled and knew that my organizational efforts were working.

However, as with "the best laid plans of mice and men," there will be times when you are not able to adhere to a schedule; the bulletin will not be typed on the designated day. When that happens, should you accept late items? By all means. People always take precedence over processes (more about that in the next chapter). If you can do so without scolding, you might remind the person that normally the bulletin would have been done by this time. You may even find people who did not know that you type the bulletin on the same day each week.

If you are the only person in your office, you may find it difficult to block out periods of time for a particular job because of the number of interruptions. Carry the analysis of your log one step further: How long would it take to type and run the bulletin if you had no interruptions? Two hours at the most? Why not ask a volunteer to serve as receptionist for that period of time? Within every congregation are willing workers—widows, senior citizens, young mothers with school-age children—who can be of invaluable assistance for short periods of time if only asked.

Some additional suggestions may help you make this scheduling work:

1. It may seem that every day is equally hectic, but within every office schedule are times that are slightly less busy. Find those times and use them for scheduling concentrated work.
2. If possible, schedule those blocks when the pastor is most likely to be away from the office or is in a period of study. By the way, helping the pastor set aside a regular time of study, free of all interruptions except those of a life-and-death nature, is one of your most important tasks.
3. If you are able to secure a volunteer, give that person a time when you will return any calls. And then do it! Build a reputation for dependability in every area.

The second step in the analysis of your log is to determine priorities. Indicate those tasks that demand immediate attention. How often do they occur? Is it possible to predict any of them? A good example is the call reporting the illness of a member. These calls are priority items—they come in every day or every week; they require immediate attention; the only variable is the number of calls. How do you handle such calls? Do you tend to jot them down on a scrap piece of paper and hope and pray the scrap doesn't get lost in the heap before you remember to tell the pastor? Because, of course, the heap already contains several other reminders of varying degrees of importance. Why not prepare an illness/hospital call-in sheet, such as that on page 126 of Part II? Keep this sheet on your desk in a labeled folder. When a report of illness comes in, reach for the folder and record the necessary information. If the folder is left on your desk, the pastor will have access to it at all times.

Many of the things you do can be categorized and organized so that you are saving everyone's time, most importantly your own. Use folders freely in your organizational efforts. Other pertinent labels might be:

a. Work to Be Done—Pastor
b. Work to Be Done—Committees
c. Work to Be Done—Board of Trustees/Session
d. Work Completed—(for the same groups)
e. Miscellaneous

Within the first four (a—d), determine the order in which you will handle the work—by date received or by importance—and maintain that order within the folder. Indicate on the incoming work any completion deadlines.

The miscellaneous folder is a necessary evil in most offices. However, either it will control you or you will control it. Review its contents at least once each day, removing items to more specific places for action or handling the matter.

Another advantage to folders is that their usage encourages confidentiality. In many church offices the secretary's desk is in a very open spot; items on the desk are easily and quickly read. Many people will read openly accessible information, but most people will not open a folder in order to satisfy their curiosity.

Your particular job will suggest many more labels or categories. Remember, your goal is to develop an organizational scheme that works so well for you that it ultimately frees the pastor from details.

A final item in the secretary's organizational efforts is the use of a tickler file. It is interesting to note that this file derives its name from the accounting term *tick*, meaning to *check off*. The tickler is a record of work to be done on future dates. The items are ticked or checked when completed. Some secretaries use their desk calendars for this purpose. The disadvantage of the calendar is that space is limited. Others prefer to keep a 3" x 5" card system, arranged by months and days. A card is placed after each date, indicating work to be done, such as meetings to be arranged, deliveries to be expected, or reports to be typed.

Need I remind you that the key to the success of the tickler or of any reminder system is the secretary's use of it on a daily basis? Incidentally, reminders should always be one-directional—from you to the pastor. If reminders are frequently moving in the other direction, something is amiss!

To complete the discussion of your professional role, consideration must be given to the personal aspect. Realistically, your professional role is either enhanced or diminished by the personal element. The success of your personal role is dependent upon three factors:

1. Your appearance
2. Your attitude
3. Your allegiance

Your appearance. Appropriate dress for today's working woman is a popular topic for writers. While much of what is written is interesting, little of it is applicable to the woman whose time, inclinations, and financial resources are limited. Hopefully, this discussion will be a more practical one. The intent is to provide you with guidelines that you can use over a period of time.

In addition, dress is a very personal matter, and any one who attempts to dictate taste to another runs the risk of either angering or turning off the reader. At the same time, appropriate dress is of vital importance to the success of the church secretary, and some attempt must be made to reach a common ground.

First, the organizational skills you have developed as a secretary will be very helpful as you analyze your appearance.

The first step in this process is to assess your present wardrobe. Separate wearables from unwearables, based on such factors as fit, length, and style. Discard those items that are no longer usable, even if this means that you are left with a bare minimum. Anne Ortlund has coined a phrase that is especially applicable here: "eliminate and concentrate."[2] Also, make any necessary repairs on wearable items. Every item hanging in your closet should be ready to put on!

Second, list your present wardrobe by item and by color. Cluster items that can or do go together. Check those for which you have the necessary accessories. Do you have "mish-mash" or "mix and match"? You should now have a total picture of the number of outfits you own that are appropriate for work, and you are ready for the third step.

Plan your future wardrobe acquisitions around your existing wardrobe. Make a personal shopping list. Add basic items first—a skirt or suit in a solid color for which you can vary the tops, for example. Unless you have an extensive wardrobe, work with one or two basic colors. Most importantly, do not stray from your shopping plan until you do have a basic wardrobe.

This raises the next question: What is appropriate dress for the church office? "Appropriate" and "modest" are synonymous in this instance. Modesty includes both fit and style. Let me suggest a thirty-second test before you leave home in the morning. Stand in front of a full-length mirror. Bend slightly forward. View yourself both front and rear. Are both views satisfactory? These are the views that

[2] Anne Ortlund, *Disciplines of the Beautiful Woman* (Waco, Texas: Word, Inc., 1977).

others have of you as you work at your desk or bend over to pick up something.

As a side note, does your mirror reveal other things you really don't like? A few extra pounds? Sloppy makeup? An outdated hairdo? Even a crooked hem? Why not do something about those things *today?* The first step in achieving an organized office is to start with yourself. Set some realistic, attainable goals for yourself, and work systematically to achieve them.

A second problem in appropriateness that many of us have as females is that we like pretty things—and rightfully so. However, as working women, we face a dichotomy: our own taste preferences and our professional images. Several studies have revealed that the style of dress of the secretary does affect the amount of confidence she projects. The more tailored the clothes, the more classical the lines, the greater the confidence that is inspired. We may have to learn to confine our love of lace to our slips! Save your prettiest dress for Sunday morning and other special occasions.

Finally, there are items of clothing and style that are of questionable appropriateness for the office. The inherent danger in trying to list these is that fashion changes so rapidly. However, perhaps the following suggestions pertinent to the early eighties will have carryover to other items as fashion dictates in the coming years.

1. *Sleeveless dresses and blouses.* These are not a firm "no" but are questionable as office wear. Sleeved items are definitely preferable. Do a candid appraisal of yourself in a sleeveless garment and then decide. If you don't like what you see, why not make one or two short-sleeved jackets in complimentary colors?
2. *Tank/sun tops, sundresses.* These are definitely out as office wear. Save them for the beach and for picnics.

3. *Pants*. Pants are a "no." Great for cleaning house and shopping, but passé for the office.
4. *Bare Legs*. Temperature notwithstanding, hose are a must in the office.

This discussion does not include your personal hygiene habits because it is assumed that you are meticulously clean. If you have any tendencies to be even the least careless in these habits because you think no one notices, I can assure you that you are wrong. These are the things that even your best friend won't tell you. Enough said?

Your attitude. The proper attitude of you, the church secretary, toward your pastor can be summed up in one word—respect. That includes respect for him as a Christian and as a person. If total respect is lacking or impossible because of any set of circumstances, it is questionable whether you can perform effectively in your role.

However, do not confuse respect with perfection. Several of the secretaries I surveyed mentioned that finding out that their pastors were human was one of the most difficult adjustments they had to make to their jobs. But pastors are human. They, like you and me, have their "down" days, their irritable days, their preoccupied days, and their impatient days. Somehow we can accept these behaviors in anyone except the pastor. That's unfair! They have all of the pressures of day-to-day living that everyone else has and, in addition, the impossible expectations of people.

On occasion your pastor may comment about another person or situation. You may feel that the remark is out of character. At such times try to see the total picture. It may have been said in a moment of exasperation. There has to be an escape valve for the pressure—and you may provide that release just by listening. Your only reaction should be to forget what was said. Even if forgetting is difficult, repeating the remark to anyone is inexcusable.

Your allegiance. The final area in which you can truly fulfill your role as a complement to the pastor's efforts is in your allegiance. This sense of loyalty should naturally evolve from the attitude of respect just discussed.

Several of the surveyed secretaries cited the difficulty of having so many bosses. One said, "650 members and 650 bosses." Many of you could echo that sentiment. It is true; you do have many bosses. You work with and for many people, but the focus of your allegiance must center in one person—the pastor.

That pastor is never going to please everyone. On any day of the week there are unhappy members, critical members, and even angry members in the best of churches. Often you will be the sounding board for these disgruntled people because you are the closest they can come to criticizing the pastor. Happy is the secretary who has learned to let these comments flow in one ear and out the other.

Not only are you not obligated to respond to pastoral criticism—personal opinions are out of place. You might lovingly say, "Have you prayed for the pastor today?"

There are times when critical remarks are potentially the sparks for explosive, divisive controversies. If you sense this, your loyalty will also require that you share this information with your pastor confidentially. There should be no surprises in his world that you could have averted.

EACH PART HELPS . . .

In your relationships and in your roles, you and the pastor are a team—"each part in its own special way helps the other parts" (Eph. 4:16, TLB). Then when you move conceptually from these two parts of the body of Christ to the larger body or to the total church family, the uniqueness of your role as a "buffer zone" becomes evident.

3
ONE OF THE FAMILY

Each of us is a part of the one body of Christ 1 Cor.
12:13a, TLB

If, at some point in the future, I am asked what I will
remember most about the executive pastor of my church,
Rev. L. Edward Davis, it will be his insistence upon
"people before processes."

A church secretary asked me, "How can I show a Christian attitude toward everyone?" Another one inquired,
"How do I keep peace between members having a difference?" Many others asked for assistance in "handling
people." And so it goes. The church secretary who cannot
formulate at least one question in this area of human relationships is indeed rare, perhaps even unique. The dual
nature of the dilemma is that the processes must be accomplished without sacrificing the needs of the people. The
total answer can only come as we look first at our responsibilities as Christians and then at our responsibilities as
secretaries.

On first reading, this approach may appear to be "Pol-
lyanna." However, the older I become, the more I realize

how often we attack problems without first drawing upon our most important resource—our faith.

Consider first the scriptural basis for our existence as a church. Just as we discussed the pastor and the secretary as parts of the body of Christ, needful of each other, so must we begin this discussion with a look at that body:

> *Our bodies have many parts, but the many parts make up only one body when they are all put together. So it is with the "body" of Christ* (1 Cor. 12:12, TLB).

Yes, even that most bothersome member of your congregation is a part of that body and has a unique contribution to make.

Just in case we have difficulty accepting that fact, Paul goes on in the twelfth chapter of Corinthians to remind us that we cannot reject any one part: ". . . each one of you is a separate and necessary part of it" (v. 27, TLB). That's quite an order, isn't it? However, if we can somehow begin to view people as having distinctive and necessary contributions to make to the larger body, that perception will have a profound effect on how we handle our processes.

Let me give you an example. While you may say it is only a matter of semantics, we speak of needing assistance in "handling" people and "handling" interruptions. Does not the use of the word "handle" imply that we want to learn how to control the situation or the person? Does it not also imply that people and interruptions are viewed as problems? Do we indeed have the proverbial cart before the horse? Can we really view people as problems if we are accepting them as needed parts of the body of Christ? Should we not rather begin to look for ways of working *with* people and *with* interruptions?

Second, our ability to work with all people will only develop as we act from a base of Christian love. That love is mandated:

. . . love one another . . . (Rom. 13:8, KJV).

> *And God himself has said that one must love not only God, but his brother too* (1 John 4:21, TLB).

That love is tested:

> *But if a person isn't loving and kind, it shows that he doesn't know God—for God is love* (1 John 4:8, TLB).

That love must be your motivating force. It doesn't just happen. Such love is clearly a gift of the Holy Spirit.

My Grandmother McKenna was truly a living saint; I never heard her say an unkind word about anyone. But I do recall a lady in our church who managed to keep things stirred up much of the time. And I also recall my grandmother's saying, "I pray more over Mrs. X than any other person I know." That's what it's all about.

I challenge you to pray, "Lord, help me love _____" (naming the person who disturbs you most). Two cautions: (1) That will be one of the most difficult prayers you will ever pray. Most of us really don't want to love everyone; our biases are too dear. (2) Don't pray that prayer unless you really mean it because the Holy Spirit will work a miracle in your life. You will find love and tolerance for that person to a degree you never dreamed possible. Then, and only then, will you be able to show a Christian attitude toward everyone.

Remember, you are in the "people business." They are your reason for being, even the difficult ones. As a result, completing a process must never take precedence over saving a person. Given that love, how then can you implement it in a practical way?

Our discussion will again center on two areas: people, specifically members; and processes. The two are necessarily interrelated but never out of order. Let's begin.

RESPONDING TO NEED

A major area of consideration for working with people is responding to need—spiritual, physical, and social/emotional. As a preliminary step in responding to those needs, the church secretary should know, by name and appearance, as many of the members as possible. A secretary cannot afford to say, "Oh, I'm terrible with names." Develop a systematic way of getting to know people. Set a realistic goal for learning a predetermined number of people each week. If you are new in your position, you may wish to start with the church leaders because you are likely to have early contact with them. Don't stop there, however. Recognize whole families. Greet people by name, for reinforcement. If you tend to confuse two persons, develop a memory crutch: "The *R*edhead is *R*uth." Introduce yourself to persons you do not recognize. Sit with a longtime member in worship services and quietly ask the names of those entering whom you do not know. Then, when needs or crises arise in member families, you will be responding to people rather than mere names.

As mentioned earlier, responding to needs will usually fall into one of three areas: spiritual, physical, or social/emotional. The church must provide a support system for all of these. Specifically, where do you, the church secretary, fit into that system?

You function primarily as the liaison between the source of the information and the source for meeting the need. You must be careful to ascertain all facts accurately, pass on the information as soon as possible, and perhaps provide temporary support for the caller without offering an opinion or making a commitment of time, resources, or personnel.

FULFILLING THE ROLE

What specific roles do you have then in each of the indicated areas of need?

Spiritual needs are very personal and may be difficult to identify specifically. They may be demonstrated in other forms of behavior: a critical spirit, an absence from worship, a lack of interest in church functions, as examples. In every instance they are complex and are best worked, talked, and prayed through with the person most qualified by training and experience to deal with them—the pastor. If a member chooses to share a spiritual need with you, you will, of course, respond with an understanding ear. You may wish to assure the person of your prayer support. However, your primary function is to move that person along to the pastor for counseling.

Physical needs are more easily identified and have two characteristics:

1. They can be met with some tangible response.
2. They vary greatly in levels of urgency; thus, the responses vary also. Variety of responses should not be synonymous with capriciousness in responses.

In fact, the church office procedure for dealing with health crises—illness (home and hospital), accident, and death—should be firmly established and followed. All persons involved should be familiar with the procedure. The church cannot afford to let even one of these "slip through the cracks." Again, specific suggestions for relaying information appear later in this chapter. Most importantly, however, you must remember that these crises occur in every church on a regular basis. They are never "interruptions" in your day or your routine but rather are your day and your routine and should be anticipated.

The other physical needs that come into the church office cannot so easily be categorized. Some can be planned for, and some will be "firsts." In any event, the church should have certain persons designated who are willing to help find the resources for meeting these needs. They may be elected officials, such as deacons, or they may be volunteers who have the time and interest to give to this ministry—and buying a bag of groceries is a ministry! The important fact is that this frees the pastor to carry on his ministry. As a point of information, the pastor should be informed of such needs and how they were met. He may then choose to make a followup call; but it's exciting to think what can happen when he can call as a pastor, after members of the congregation have already met the physical needs of one of their own.

Likewise, the social/emotional needs of the members differ greatly in urgency and nature, and the responses will vary appropriately. In many cases, they require the services of an expert. That expert may be the pastor, or it may be a referral agency. Leave that decision to the pastor.

Even though your role in this area of people needs is primarily that of liaison, an inordinate proportion of your time is spent in listening to people; consequently, you cannot be overtrained or too knowledgeable in these skills. There are many excellent books available for developing and refining your people-helping abilities. I would recommend that each of you establish a regular reading habit, even a few minutes a day, studying available materials. The typewriter is an object; it can be used to relay the information regarding an illness or a death within the congregation, but only the person operating the typewriter can "reach out and touch someone" who is in pain (my apologies to the Bell System!).

SERVING AS GO-BETWEEN

However, there are times when you must function as a mediator. In that capacity you occupy a tenuous position. On the one hand, you are the person who is going to hear the criticism of one member toward another, toward the church, or toward the minister. You want to be the "eyes and ears" of the church in order to convey those comments or concerns that can be helpful in building the church. And yet, you do not want to be considered a sounding board for every petty gripe members have. What should you do? You can't play ostrich and bury your head in the sand. When you come up for air, the problem will still be there.

Unfortunately, there are no magic formulas that can be applied to every instance of criticism. So much depends on the person doing the criticizing and the object of the criticism. You must examine all the facts before relaying any information on to the church staff. Ask yourself: Could something have been done differently? Could someone have acted or reacted differently? Can something positive come out of the negative? Who is voicing the criticism? Is this person really masking some deeper problems?

There are a few suggestions that may be helpful in dealing with this problem:

1. Don't take sides—even when you have "a side." The least evidence of support will only spur some people on to repeated, more emotional performances.

2. Don't offer advice. If you see a way of building a bridge between the differences, you might do so. Or if you can correct false information, without revealing a confidence, you might do that. Any action on your part requires careful and prayerful judgment.

3. If you must respond, develop the art of answering a negative comment with a positive one. Remember, a soft answer still turns away wrath.

4. Or, if you must relay the criticism to others, try to give the criticism a positive aspect also.

Differences between people need not always be totally negative experiences. The first step in the formal problem-solving process is to identify the problem. The second step is to gather all the facts. The third step, then, is to use those facts to identify the real problem in order to arrive at possible solutions. Let me use an example.

Recently a member of a prominent church in our area shared with me an incident in which one of the deacons of that church failed to respond to a physical need of a member. "Failure to respond" was the immediate, identifiable problem; hurt feelings were the immediate result. However, as we explored all of the facts, we learned that the real problem was quite different. The deacon in question had not been asked to respond to a single need as she had done many times in the past. Rather, she was expected to assume leadership over other persons who would in turn respond to this need over a period of time. However, due to the complexity of her own personal relationships, she was incapable of assuming leadership. She was an excellent worker as long as someone else was giving the directions. Once the real problem was identified—a lack of leadership—it was possible to develop an alternative solution. Ultimately, from what began as a potentially negative situation, came a review of leadership expectations; and some long-range, positive results followed. This example need not be the unusual but can become the usual.

Criticism of the pastor must be dealt with in its own way. So much depends on the type of relationship you have with the pastor. For example, can you talk to him freely and not be misunderstood? How does he react to criticism? Can you relay criticism in a spirit of wanting to help and not wanting merely to tell? Will it affect his relationship with the criticizer? What kind of a day has it been? Perhaps, and most important, will some good result from your relaying the comment? Again, careful, prayerful judgment is in order.

Then, it is important to remember that there are members in every congregation who simply have critical spirits. The object of their criticism may vary from day to day but is just as certain as the day. Probably the best you can do is to maintain a pleasant attitude and a ready smile—even when it kills you! Such people need help; the cherished hurts they are nursing in order to maintain a critical spirit go far deeper than you can cope with. Let their comments go in one ear and out the other.

The discussion of this chapter to this point reinforces the fact that this business of working with people is always complex and requires flexibility. Then, there is one additional consideration that you, the church secretary, should keep in mind: Learning to work with people involves a process of growth. You will make mistakes; you will become irritated; you will have moments of frustration, even exasperation; you will often have to say, "I'm sorry." All of these reactions are a part of the process. Use each of your feelings of failure as building blocks for future situations. Start each day fresh, determined to do a little better in this people business today than you did yesterday.

Finally, since the people aspect of your job is involved and unpredictable, it is even more important that your processes be standardized, thus adding a degree of stability to at least one part of your job.

THE PROCESSES

The results of the secretarial survey indicate that the processes for working with a congregation fall into five major categories:

1. Processing of information
2. Working with office/telephone callers
3. Establishing and maintaining files
4. Communicating with church leaders
5. Supervising volunteers

Let's consider each of these in order.

Processing of information. The processing of information in the church office should be described in three ways:

41

accurate, rapid, and confidential. Those adjectives can only be applied if the process you use is systematized. There is no time in your day for handling every bit of information differently. Establish a procedure and stay with it long enough to evaluate its workability. One breakdown in communication does not necessarily mean that you should scuttle the system. Determine how and where the break occurred. Can a recurrence be prevented and the system be retained? On the other hand, if several breakdowns occur, it's time to reevaluate and implement needed changes.

The following suggested procedure may serve as a basis for developing your own information system.

1. The information is received *and recorded*. Recording should not be on loose slips of paper that can easily be misplaced, but rather on standard forms. Pages 127-132 of Part II illustrate several forms that might be included in your system.
2. The information is passed on to the appropriate person as quickly as possible. The appropriate person is the pastor or his designee.
3. Any additional persons, such as deacons or visitation committee members, are notified, also as appropriate.
4. The records are then completed by making notations of each of the above actions. Thus, at all times, the status of the situation is known.
5. Appropriate followup procedures are implemented.

Briefly but thoroughly describe your procedure for the processing of information to any others who might be working with it. Then, even if you are away from your office, you retain continuity of process.

Working with office and telephone callers. Let's consider first an efficient plan for working with office callers.

Appointments should be scheduled in two books—yours

42

and the pastor's. At least once each day, check to see that the two books are in agreement. Don't expect the pastor to remember to tell you that he has added or changed an appointment—that's your job!

Then, review the day's schedule with the pastor. Be sure you have allotted ample time for each appointment. Assemble any papers the pastor may need for business appointments. Give these to him in a folder just prior to the appointment. Since you know better than anyone else the mess that accumulates on a pastor's desk in the course of a day, you'll also know why you keep the folder until he is ready to prepare for the appointment.

Two additional notations in your appointment book will often help you cope with a busy day: the telephone number of each person scheduled and a check beside the name of those who are usually willing to be "juggled" if that becomes necessary. The courtesy of a telephone call to those whose appointments are apt to be delayed is always appreciated.

As an experienced secretary, you will develop a keen sense of discrimination in this matter of callers.

Some of the people who come through your door are simply lonely. The two or three minutes you spend chatting with them is a "people investment" that pays big dividends. Have you ever asked such persons if they would like to become volunteer helpers? Coral Ridge (Fla.) Presbyterian Church has a coterie of retired persons whom they have lovingly labeled "Wonderful Willing Workers." Are you utilizing such resources in your congregation? Couldn't the hours you spend folding bulletins, stuffing envelopes, or checking attendance be used in more productive ways? Particularly if you could give another Christian a feeling of usefulness? Also, with a little ingenuity, the lonely person can be physically located near enough to hear and see people and yet far enough away to make a running conversation impossible. You are then meeting the needs of both of you.

Many members will usurp an inordinate amount of the pastor's time, if permitted to do so. Some situations require all the wits the secretary can muster to work around these. Three techniques may help:

1. Many secretaries interrupt pastoral appointments with a telephone call after a certain amount of time has passed. This is done, of course, only by prearrangement. This may provide the break the pastor needs to terminate the conversation so he can move on to other callers or other matters.
2. The caller who tends to take a lot of time should always be scheduled before another appointment. Thus, the secretary can say, "Thirty minutes are available on Tuesday at three o'clock." This, then, also provides for a legitimate breaking point.
3. The secretary should discreetly, without probing, try to ascertain the nature of the call. Many times callers are looking for information that she can provide.

You will need this same discriminatory sense when the situation is the office caller who wants to take up your time rather than the pastor's. Again, there are some approaches you may be able to use to protect your time.

First, you must never be rude. The one or two minutes it may take to greet the caller will not make or break your day.

However, if the conversation drifts from business after initial pleasantries, there are other things you might do:

1. If the caller is waiting for an appointment, offer a cup of coffee and a current Christian periodical and return to your work.
2. If it is evident that the person just wants to talk, and you wouldn't mind if you weren't busy, suggest lunch soon, explaining that you need to complete

some work at the moment. Or simply say, "Let's talk about it real soon. Why don't you give me a call tomorrow evening?"

Or, better yet, "I'll call you real soon." Then you control the time element.

Yes, there are persons in every congregation who are totally oblivious to any hints you might give. There are times when you may simply have to say, "I'm sorry, but I must get busy and finish this job." This abrupt approach should be used infrequently and with great sensitivity. Interruptions are a part of the day of any person in the "people business." They can totally frustrate you, or you can see them in perspective as indicative of the relationship that they affirm—that of people to their church.

The conversation with the telephone caller can sometimes be more difficult to terminate without appearing rude. The best way to keep the conversation brief is to keep it centered on the reason for the call. In fact, you can encourage or discourage further conversation just by your responses. If all else fails, it is amazing how much work you can do while balancing a receiver on your shoulder!

The telephone is a necessary evil. Wanting to scream if it rings "just one more time" is a common reaction. It, like people, is a part of your day and a part of your routine. You must work with its incessant ringing and not let it work on you. Again, having a systematic approach to telephone messages can help.

Some churches log in all calls, recording name of caller, time of call, person being called, etc. This then serves as a record of all telephone contacts as well as providing a point of reference for the future. A sheet from a church telephone log appears on page 125.

More commonly, a telephone message form (illustrated on page 122) is used, with the form being passed along to the appropriate person. The critical information on a telephone message is the caller's name (spelled correctly), the date and time of the call, and a brief, accurate message.

It is easy when you are busy to record telephone messages on any available piece of paper. Don't! Keep your message pad and pen next to the telephone and use it exclusively for telephone messages.

Whether your office uses the telephone log, message forms, or some other system, you must protect the confidentiality of messages at all times. Recently I walked into a church office where the secretary had arranged numerous telephone messages facing the front of her desk. Now I realize it was her intention to make it easy for each of the pastors to identify and pick up his own messages, but what about other callers who could read the messages with equal ease?

Keep the telephone log in a folder, properly labeled. If you work for one pastor, keep the message forms also in a folder or on his desk, if his desk is inaccessible to others when he is away from the office.

Finally, while each of you knows the importance of being pleasant on the telephone, sometimes it helps to be reminded. Did you know that a smile on your face is actually reflected in your telephone voice? Or does your telephone voice too often reflect the busyness of your day? Pausing just a second before picking up the receiver will remove the "edge" from your voice. Reminding yourself that, to many people, your telephone *is* your church will help you to see it as another vehicle of a total ministry.

Establishing and maintaining files. Although the needs of each church vary and the files and filing system will reflect those individual requirements, membership records seem to present the most problems to church secretaries. Membership records generally fall into three categories:

1. A working membership file
2. Permanent membership records
3. A system of family folders

First, your working file is the one that you use most frequently, even several times a day. Thus, it should be in a form that aids accessibility. Many secretaries find that a card system, particularly the rotary type, is the most accessible as well as the most convenient for recording changes.

The working file should have two categories: *Active* and *Inactive*. Ask for or suggest specific guidelines for moving a family from one category to another—nonattendance for a specified period, a move from the area, etc. Ideally, the Inactive group should be kept in the back of your card file, thereby requiring less handling when working with the file.

This business of inactive families can be a delicate one, since many pastors are reluctant to "give up" on anyone. But your action need not signify a "giving up" on the part of a loving church family. These families can still be included in mailings, calling programs, and other efforts to renew their ties to the church. The categorization simply facilitates the operations of the church office.

A third category, *Regular Attenders*, may also be desirable. Again, a specific guideline is needed for adding these families to the files. For example, you might begin a record if a family has attended worship services three times and has not indicated another church home. Hopefully, after a third visit, a contact will have been made with the family to ascertain the degree of its interest.

These three categories and a sample card are shown on page 147 of Part II.

Keep your working file free of "nice to know" information. Include only the most vital data: names, addresses, and telephone numbers. In addition, "clue" your cards for other important bits of information. The tiny stick-on dots, color coded, are easy to use. For example, a yellow dot might signify widowed persons within the congregation; red dots, young persons whose parents do not attend, and so forth. By devising and using such a system, you have information at your fingertips that can be used for better meeting the needs of the congregation.

A second major category of membership records is the permanent register. Most churches, for historical reasons, need a master membership record that includes the name of every person who has ever been a member. Again, this record should be a "clean" one, containing only that data which is vital to church records, such as date of joining, date of baptism, date and reason for leaving. This record is probably best kept in a ledger. It may be maintained alphabetically or numerically. If kept numerically, in order of joining, it should contain an alphabetical index. This record should be considered highly confidential and have extremely limited access. A sample ledger page is also shown on page 146.

The third type of membership record is the family folder. This file is literally a series of manila file folders, filed alphabetically and kept in a locked file. The file would include any questionnaire completed prior to membership, letter of transfer, baptismal dates, correspondence with the family, and any other documents containing information about the family. This file should be retained indefinitely. It will be necessary to sort out the total file periodically so that files of families no longer in the church can be moved to a permanent storage location.

Managing all of the files in the church office should also be a systematic process. As membership information is received, place it in your pending file. Set aside a portion of a specific day each month for recording changes. First, alphabetize the bits of information you have—yes, even those handwritten notes. Then, process all changes at one time, even preparing an alphabetical list of changes for the month and distributing it to appropriate people.

Use a similar procedure for maintaining the files of the office and the pastor. Try to establish the habit of filing regularly. I never met a secretary who enjoyed filing! Delaying the inevitable only compounds the problem.

Maintain correspondence files alphabetically by name of writer on incoming letters and by name of addressee on outgoing items. (A note about alphabetical files that reflect a personal bias—Mac's and Mc's are filed alphabetically within the M's—not before or after all other M's!)

The pastor will probably want a subject file also. If one is already in existence, familiarize yourself with it thoroughly. Or, if he lets you set up the file (bless him!), prepare an index that will help him locate materials quickly.

Well-organized and well-maintained files are a thing of beauty. Even if you've never seen the beauty, you do know the value of having them thus in your working day. It's worth a try. You may even wonder how you ever tolerated the confusion.

Communicating with church leaders. Whether the leadership ranks in your church number six, sixty, or more, you are going to have times when you feel you have too many bosses. In most instances, you and the pastor really do serve at the pleasure of those persons. While that relationship is constant, you can determine and maintain a positive tone for the relationship.

There are two extremes to the relationship between the secretary and the church leadership. On one end is "good ol' Gladys" who feels compelled to do everything for everybody at all times and drives herself to a frazzle in doing so. On the other end is "complaining Carrie" who spends most of her time bemoaning the amount of work she is expected to do for the amount of money she is paid. She's also very good at chastising those who fail to follow her procedures. Somewhere in between these two positions is "efficient Evelyn," your role model. How do you achieve this position? There are two personal pointers I can suggest before adding some specific procedures.

First, act *efficient* without acting *officious.* Remember, you are in control of the situation in the church office. Others are requesting your services. There is no reason for being defensive, and that is an easy posture to assume, particularly when dealing with people who tend to be overbearing.

Second, there are times in every organization, regardless of purpose or size, when the "best laid plans" fall apart. When genuine, unforeseeable emergencies arise, deal with them promptly and efficiently, foregoing all established procedures, if necessary.

The key to recognizing real emergencies is the frequency of occurrence. If a crisis occurs daily, something is wrong—and "crisis" is not equated with "unexpected." The unexpected is a part of your day and can usually be worked into your routines. Or, if emergencies typically involve the same person, then it may be time for a secretary-church leader talk. Don't enter into such a conversation with only complaints. Have some suggested solutions ready, too. It's easy to gripe; it's much more difficult to arrive at workable solutions to problems, but that's the only approach that's really worthwhile in the long run.

Now, for some specific procedures for promoting good communications between your office and church leaders.

As a beginning, establish a master calendar of church activities that you alone maintain. Insist upon your making all additions, deletions, or changes. Be pleasant but firm in this matter. If you are going to operate efficiently in such areas as meeting notices, room arrangements, preparation of materials, etc., you must have as accurate a schedule of church activities as possible. Such potential problems as two groups wanting the same room are easily solved because you know whose request was first. This fair but firm practice will work wonders in getting people to schedule early.

Then, put all work requests in writing. Devise a simple form (see page 128) for listing the needed information such as name of person making the request, date of request, date needed, number of copies, and name and phone number of person to be contacted if any additional information is needed. Whether you fill out the form or whether you ask the other person to complete it will probably depend upon the size of your church and the method with which you are most comfortable.

Using the work requests, determine priorities for your work. Every leader and every committee chairperson believes his or her work is most important. You need not convey your priorities to these people and risk offending them. Simply do it. You may arrange your work by order received, or, if possible, by importance—never by your own preferences for either the work or the people.

Finally, establish your reputation for dependability and follow through. Don't promise more than you can deliver. Work steadily and efficiently. Establish routines wherever possible. If you "goof," admit your mistake; apologize, if possible and appropriate; take steps to prevent a recurrence; and get on with your work. It happens to the best of people!

Your relationship with church leaders should develop into one of mutual respect because you both have earned it.

Supervising volunteers—a bane or a blessing? Most church offices, simply for economic reasons, could not function without volunteers. How successful the volunteer system is again depends on your management of it. If I may be presumptuous, I will offer you ten commandments for working with volunteers.

1. Don't ask volunteers to work beyond their capabilities. Determine their interests and abilities and use them in those areas.
2. Use each volunteer sparingly; in other words, don't wear out your welcome!
3. Always remember to express sincere thanks for each job done.
4. Praise the volunteer's efforts publicly whenever possible.

5. Prompt the pastor to thank volunteers periodically. For some people, one word of appreciation and recognition from him is worth many from you.

6. If a volunteer comes in to perform a task for another staff member, let the responsible person do the supervising.

7. Work at finding out each volunteer's niche and put him in it. The resources in every congregation are greater than those tapped. Grandma Jones may not be able to type a mailing list, but she can bake super cookies for that important committee meeting. (By the way, the extra cookies should go into the freezer and not into "the ministry." Then you're all set for the next meeting.)

8. Never ask a volunteer to deal with known confidential matters. If a volunteer inadvertently encounters confidential information, be very frank in explaining its nature and the importance of its not being relayed.

9. Have a "Volunteer Appreciation" recognition at least annually.

10. Try to tie down specific volunteers for specific jobs on a regular basis, i.e., folding the monthly newsletter, stuffing envelopes, etc., so you don't waste valuable time finding a person each month. You'll find that many of your volunteers are really very busy people, and they will appreciate being able to plan ahead.

IS THAT ALL?

After reading this chapter, you may, with tongue in cheek, ask: "Is that all she expects of me? Super interpersonal relationships and completely organized processes? It sounds more like the Great Church Office in the Sky than mine."

No, I have great respect for the tremendous job that many of you are doing under less than ideal conditions. However, if you can remind yourself that all good relationships take time to develop and all good processes require trial and error, you can also change your world—even a little at a time.

BRIDGING⁴ THE GAP

I looked in vain for anyone . . . who could stand in the gap . . . Ezek. 22:30, TLB

The idea for this book first came to me on an occasion when I called for information from a church with which I had no previous contacts. The curtness of the secretary who answered the telephone made me realize just how important that initial impression is. I wondered what my response would have been if I had been a timid soul who had just worked up the courage to place such a call. Or, I reflected on how I might have responded to the lack of warmth if I had been a person in serious emotional trouble. Fortunately, I was neither; and, hopefully, persons calling your office will never need to ask themselves those questions.

This chapter then will discuss those "people and process" concerns, other than those of the pastor and members, that are a part of your outreach responsibilities.

THE PEOPLE

Your people contacts are primarily of three types: office callers, telephone callers, and visitors to church services.

Correspondence from nonmembers, another source of people contacts, can be handled more easily than the first two types mentioned because there is time to think about an appropriate response. This is not so with people standing in front of your desk or being on the other end of your telephone. Since many of the telephone techniques discussed in the previous chapter can also be applied to conversations with nonmembers, let's begin with a discussion of those persons who come into your office.

First, there are those who are a part of your "extended" church family—former members, relatives of members, nonattending parents of Sunday school youths, occasional attenders, and others. How should you respond when they encounter crises and enlist the help of the church?

It is very helpful if your church or pastor has established a policy for working with nonmembers in crises. In the smaller church the pastor is usually very willing to respond in any way he can during such times. He accepts this opportunity as a part of the total outreach ministry. In larger churches, where the pastoral load may be extremely heavy, other persons may have to be asked to be of assistance. In any situation, work toward developing a pattern of responses so that each crisis does not precipitate a larger crisis within your office.

How do you say "No" to such persons when and if you must? Try to avoid an outright "No" and then a dropping of the matter. Rather make every effort to see if alternatives are available. For example, one secretary told me she had recently been receiving an unusual number of phone calls requesting transportation, both to church services and to other places. There was no set provision for providing such within her church organizational structure. So while she must convey this fact, she also offered to pass such requests along to an appropriate person, who posted a notice on the church bulletin board. Thus, a totally negative answer was avoided.

Is she ever criticized by the caller? Of course, and you

will be too whenever you must say "No." It really is one of those "no win — only lose" situations. Your shoulders just have to be a little broader at times. That's not much consolation, but it's so true!

Second, it seems that in these times a variety of people are attracted to the church and what it represents. Unfortunately, this attraction is not always prompted by the purest of motives. This is best illustrated by a recent experience I had.

On a Saturday morning I stopped into my church office to distribute some materials. As I entered the office, I noticed the secretary was talking to a young man. She then called to me, "Pat, can you help me locate a dentist for this young man? He's in great pain." I suggested two or three names. While she continued to make telephone calls, the young man told me a very convincing story. However, since it was a Saturday morning, she was unable to locate a dentist. The matter was quite forgotten until a few days later when my husband and I were guests at a dinner party which included a local dentist. I started to tell him of this experience when he interrupted me and said, "Let me finish your story." To my amazement he did so with great accuracy. He then told me that the pained expression and sad story were ones of considerable experience and were, in fact, ploys to obtain pain-killing drugs. You can imagine the surprise of the church secretary when I relayed to her this most recent experience.

It so happens that this particular secretary is tops in the "people business," and dropping everything else to help a total stranger is second nature to her, as it is to many of you. However, she will use this latest experience to be a little more discriminating in future situations. She is not alone. Each of you must also sharpen your skills of discernment. You occupy a vulnerable position.

"Drop in" needs can be very convincing. The one thing you can share without cost is love. At the same time it is probably not wise to turn your world upside down until the pastor has had an opportunity to talk with the person. Being a skeptic is not an easy role for many of you. You will make mistakes in judgment. You may be criticized by those who disagree with "spot" decisions. Your only defense need be that your errors were prompted by a sense of genuine Christian love.

The third type of nonmember office caller is the person who wishes to interview the minister. This can particularly be a problem if he enjoys any prominence at all. In most cases you are going to have to be the guardian of his time and refuse most such requests. As an alternative, you may be able to provide much of the information the person is seeking. Do so if you can and if it is appropriate. Or, if you feel the request is justified, you might ask the person to write down the three or four most important questions and offer to have the answers within a few days. This provides an opportunity for you to either draft some answers for the pastor's perusal or ask the pastor to make some notes in response to the questions from which you can prepare the answers. In either case you will have saved valuable interview time.

Then, there is the business caller. Be pleasant in ascertaining the exact nature of the call. Ask for a business card. Rarely should such a person see the pastor on a first call. If you think his product or service may be of interest to the pastor, learn all you can about it, taking careful notes. Relay the information to the pastor. Then, if he is genuinely interested, schedule an appointment.

Another group of persons with whom you will do business is service people. If you call for repairs on your own equipment, be specific in describing the problem. If possible, have a sample of the faulty product. When others on your staff place the calls, encourage them to notify you also so you can quickly refer the repair person to the proper location. You will find that your church will receive more efficient service on future calls if you have a reputation for an efficient in-house operation.

Whoever the office caller is, your job is to convey a pleasant, interested attitude. If you are on the phone when a visitor enters, acknowledge the person's presence by a nod, a smile, or an uplifted finger. Thank the person for waiting, and offer to be of assistance. If the person appears uneasy, take extra care to put him at ease. At that moment you are "the church." That realization will have a bearing on your ability to respond properly.

Last but certainly not least is another group of nonmembers that is very important to you—the visitors to worship services. Each visiting person represents a great opportunity for your church to show how much it cares.

Every visitor to your church should experience two things: A personal welcome from members at the time of attendance and a followup contact. As church secretary, you probably have little or nothing to do with seeing that visitors are personally welcomed at services. However, you can and should have much to do with making the followup contacts.

Followup of visitors can take many forms—from a printed postcard, the least personal approach but still a contact—to a personal telephone call or visit from the pastor or his designee. Out-of-town visitors and local visitors may also be treated differently. The postcard approach may be fine for the out-of-towner, while this is only a starting point for the local visitor. Whatever your system is, it should have these characteristics.

1. Every visitor should be contacted in some way. If you do not have a systematic plan for accomplishing this, one should be established and implemented immediately.
2. Letters of welcome should be personally typed and signed; form letters are too uncaring. If you have to send out many letters of welcome, you may be able to have the letters run off on an offset press.

You can then insert the name and address, almost without detection.

3. A record of visitors should be kept. The postcard should be sent only once to a person. When that person has visited two or three times, another more personal letter should follow.

4. When a visitor continues to attend, the pastor should be notified for his personal followup.

5. Keeping track of visitors is an excellent task for a volunteer to assume.

THE PROCESSES

Those processes that have impact beyond your immediate church family are centered in your products — correspondence, bulletins, news releases, and newsletters being the most common.

Correspondence samples and guides are included in the Appendix, so this discussion will cover other typing that you do. Since the church bulletin is a weekly responsibility, the preparation of it should be standardized as much as possible. Establish a regular time of the week when you are going to type it. Plan your work schedule accordingly. Yes, there will be interruptions; but preparation of the bulletin will have top priority during this time, other than emergencies. In fact, a further recommendation is that you plan this time to be no later than Thursday of each week. In this way you are allowing time for actual emergencies that may delay you. Set your deadline for receiving items for the bulletin at least one-half day prior to your typing time, and stick to it! Thus, you have time to sort and edit items and plan the layout. If possible, schedule a volunteer to answer the phone while you are typing. This will minimize your interruptions and greatly assist you in getting done quickly.

Then, a related matter — your typewriter. At some point your typewriter will need to be replaced (too often, only when it has become a museum piece!). My first recommendation is that you select elite (twelve-pitch) type. This smaller type facilitates layouts and is more attractive on half sheets such as bulletins and executive-size stationery. If budget is not a severe problem, then it is an excellent investment to purchase a dual pitch machine. Thus, you will also have access to the larger pica (ten-pitch) type, particularly for children's materials.

Incidentally, be brave in this matter of selecting a typewriter. Even though Joe Strongarm, chairman of the board, recommends a super bargain he saw advertised at the local discount store, stand your ground, and insist upon being a part of the selection process. You, not Joe, have to use the typewriter. It represents an investment, not merely a purchase. Spending a few additional dollars may buy you added years of use while minimizing service problems. Above all, do not buy a typewriter that you cannot try out first for a few days in your own office. A reputable dealer is happy to give you a demonstration model for this purpose. And don't forget to cut a stencil while you have it!

Cover your typewriter when you leave the office for the day. Tape a note to the cover, politely asking others not to use the typewriter. You may be labeled "Wanda Witch," but you'll get better service out of your machine.

The actual typing of the bulletin can be facilitated by your keeping a back copy with all tab stops marked that you use each week. Why backspace these each time? For example, if your church name is not printed on the outside, your sample might look like the one on page 62.

The schedule of activities should be the same as that shown on your master calendar. You may need to add such information as meeting room or materials needed.

"Bulletin" and "announcement" are synonymous terms. Use that as your clue and restrict the bulletin to "announcements"—order of worship, the week's activities, illnesses, bereavements, and other pertinent information.

center point
33
22
UNITED DISCIPLES CHURCH
24
Anytown, State 00000
23
Sunday, December 25, 1980
25
9:30 and 11:00 a.m.

5
(Left Margin)

62
(Right Margin)

Other items should be reserved for the church newsletter.

Must you include artwork in your bulletin? Probably not, unless you are particularly talented in this area and can produce it in a minimum amount of time. An accurately typed, well-arranged bulletin can be equally attractive without artwork.

On the other hand, if you or others in your church do use a lot of artwork, I recommend looking into the possibility of purchasing an electronic stencil maker. You can reproduce a variety of items in greater quantities quickly and easily. In addition, the copy is typed or prepared on regular bond paper, which facilitates making corrections.

The second major typing production you prepare is the church newsletter. If you are not presently publishing a newsletter, begin to make plans to do so. Whether you are in a small church and find that bimonthly or even quarterly issues are sufficient, or in a large church where a monthly publication is desired, the newsletter is one more means of communicating and building a feeling of mutual support within the family. Just as each of us loves to hear from other members of our families, we should nurture the feeling of belonging to a particular family or congregation as a part of the larger family of God.

The church newsletter is an excellent item for utilizing an interested volunteer. A person who will gather informa-

tion, draft and/or edit that information, and plan the layout
can save you valuable time. You can and should retain
editorial rights and do a final proofing before the newsletter is printed. Thus, you control both content and accuracy.

What can be included in your newsletter? The possibilities are endless. The one guideline that should govern
inclusion is: Does the article fit into our objective: Promoting growth within the church family. Within that broad
goal then are several subgoals as shown on the following
suggested list.

Lead Article: "From the Pastor's Study . . ."

A short letter from the pastor to his people. This is an
opportunity for the pastor to share some thoughts of the
season or concerns of particular importance to his congregation.

Keeping the Family Informed
   Calendar of events
   Sunday school report
   Women's association reports
   Children's and/or youth group reports
Knowing Each Other Better
   People profiles: leaders, new members, any members,
      Senior Spotlight, youths
   A listing of visitors
Encouraging the Family to Share
   Thank you notes
   Notices of needs
Nurturing the Family
   Theme for devotionals or Bible readings for the month
   Book reviews by members

This listing is by no means exhaustive. It is only intended
to start your thinking. You will develop your own list as you
find those items that are most meaningful to your "family."

An accuracy reminder to you—when typing either the

bulletin or the newsletter, double check all facts. Proofread carefully. If you are in doubt about the correct spelling of a person's name, ask for the correct spelling. Then follow through by verifying that your records have the correct spelling. It should not be necessary to ask a second time. By the way, if your own spelling ability is less than it should be, ask another person to proofread your materials before they are printed. Begin your own spelling glossary. As you are aware that a certain word gives you trouble, list it in your glossary and refer to it as often as necessary. Being a weak speller is no disgrace; doing nothing to improve your skills is!

The third item that you are apt to be asked to type is a news release. In many cases you will only need to call the local newspaper and ask for the church news editor. Have all the facts together before you place the call. Typically, the newspaper person will then write the article.

However, your being expected to compose and submit a news release should also be accepted as normal routine. Some hints for accomplishing this are:

1. A news item is not the place for flowery language. Be direct, almost terse. Present the facts first. Then add any background information. Newspaper editors "cut" from the bottom up.
2. Double space your copy (see page 101 of Part II).
3. Date the news release, including both the date of submitting and the date of release.
4. Know your newspaper's deadlines and adhere to them.
5. Submit every item of vital interest. Be the church that the community knows because it is publicized so often.

STANDING IN THE GAP

You are the first point of contact for many people. If it all depends on you, will that contact be the first of many or the last of any? You can influence that decision by determining to be the person "standing in the gap." That gap is best filled by a quiet, efficient, and consistent demonstration of the love of Christ flowing through people employed by his church.

Part Two

THE
PROCESSES

5
THE SECRETARY'S TOOLS

Your job is either made easier or more difficult by the quality of the tools with which you work. This section provides information that will help you select the most appropriate tools for your job.

THE TYPEWRITER

The standard type-bar electric typewriter is gradually being replaced by the single-element machine. (Some sources report that 80 percent of all office typewriter sales are now the single-element machine.) There are many reasons for this, but three of the more apparent ones are:

1. Relatively little maintenance is required.
2. No jamming of keys is possible, and there is less vibration while typing.
3. A variety of type sizes and styles are available.

If you have a machine with a type basket and carriage, you will need to brush the basket frequently. Always brush toward yourself. Also, be sure to read the manufacturer's instructions before applying oil or other fluids to any parts of your typewriter. Cover your machine at the end of the day.

Type sizes and styles. In addition to the standard ten- and twelve-pitch type[1] styles, other types are available for special work. Four such styles available in twelve-pitch type are illustrated here. Similar types are available in ten-pitch.

TYPE	TYPE	TYPE	TYPE
Prestige	Courier	Gothic	*Script*

Ribbons. The quality of your typewriter ribbon is a reflection of the importance you attach to the appearance of your work. The following chart is included to help you select the most appropriate ribbon for the work you do.

Type of Ribbon	Quality of Ribbon	Quality of Image	Advantages	Disadvantages
Carbon (mylar or polyethylene)	Best available	Sharp, printlike	Thinnest Strongest Breakfree Lintfree Eliminates need to clean type	Most expensive
Fabric (silk or nylon)	Finest of fabric ribbons	Clear Sharp	Lintfree Longer life Available in grades of inking	
Fabric (cotton)	Many grades available	Dependent on grade	Less expensive Shorter life than other fabric ribbons	Leaves lint on keys

CORRECTION SUPPLIES

Knowing when and how to make undetectable corrections is the mark of the master typist. Unless you are fortunate enough to have one of the newer correcting typewriters, producing undetectable errors is one of your more important tasks. Several correcting devices are available.

[1]Ten- and twelve-pitch type styles refer to the number of typing spaces per inch.

Eraser

1. Use a clean typing (ink) eraser for originals. You can keep your typing eraser clean by rubbing it on an emery board.
2. Use a soft (pencil) eraser for carbon copies.
3. Use an erasing shield (a metal or plastic card with a variety of openings) to protect the rest of your work. Place the shield over the error and, using short vertical strokes, erase through the opening.
4. Place a card *in front of* the first carbon sheet before erasing. This preserves your carbon for additional use and eliminates the possibility of forgetting to remove little slips of paper. Use the same procedure for multiple carbons.

If the carbon copy is only for your files, it is generally no longer corrected.

Correction fluid. If the appearance of the original is important, do not use correction fluid. If, however, the original is to be used for making photocopies, this is a good correction device.

Apply correction fluid sparingly, being careful not to get it on any parts of the typewriter. Touch it on; do not brush it on. When the fluid has dried slightly, type the correction.

Correction paper. Correction paper is used most effectively when the correct letter is the same size and shape as the error. It is also used best on good quality stationery. Some corrections made with correction paper are detectable, so it should be used sparingly.

Correction tape. Correction tape comes in strips the same size as a line of single-spaced type and is self-adhering. While it makes very fine corrections if the original is being used only for photocopying, it should not be used if the original is to be mailed or distributed.

STATIONERY

Frequently church offices select stationery of inferior quality hoping to convey the impression that the people's money is being spent prudently. Too often it is forgotten that members, in all sizes of churches, like to be proud of their church. At the same time, little thought is given to the secretary's efforts to produce professional-looking correspondence with second-rate tools. While a high-quality paper is most desirable, medium qualities are available that can truly enhance the image of the church and make the secretary's job easier. Contact a reliable printer when making your choice.

Letterheads. The letterhead used by your office should be printed on good quality bond paper. A sixteen-pound weight is preferable.

The letterhead should appear within the top two inches of the sheet and should be simple. If a logo is included, it should be small, attractive, and meaningful. A very simple letterhead is illustrated here.

UNITED DISCIPLES CHURCH

100 Main Street

Anytown, State 00000

I. M. Goodwill, Th.D.   Telephone: (000) 123-4567

While stationery is available in many sizes, the three sizes most frequently used are:

Standard	8½ x 11 inches
Executive	7¼ x 10½ inches
Baronial	5½ x 8½ inches

```
┌─────────────────────────────────────────────┐
│ Standard                                      │
│   ┌───────────────────────────────────────┐  │
│   │ Executive                             │  │
│   │                                       │  │
│   │      ┌────────────────────────────┐   │  │
│   │      │ Baronial                   │   │  │
│   │      │                            │   │  │
│   │      │                            │   │  │
│   │      │                            │   │  │
│   │      │                            │   │  │
│   │      │                            │   │  │
│   │      │                            │   │  │
│   │      │                            │   │  │
│   │      │                            │   │  │
│   │      └────────────────────────────┘   │  │
└───┴──────────────────────────────────────┴──┘
```

Standard is the most frequently used size for business correspondence.

Executive is used by the pastor for personal business correspondence.

Baronial is used for very short letters.

If your church budget is limited and you are unable to stock all three sizes, you should purchase in the following order: *standard, baronial,* and *executive.*

Plain paper of the same size and quality as the letterhead is used for second and succeeding pages.

In addition, a supply of inexpensive paper should be maintained for draft copy.

ENVELOPES

Envelopes should be the same quality and color as the letterhead and should be the appropriate size for the stationery being used.

The following suggestions for typing envelope addresses should be helpful to you.

1. *Placement of addresses:*
   Small envelopes (No. 6¾). Begin typing the address on line 12 from the top and at 30 (pica) or at 35 (elite).
   Large envelopes (No. 10). Begin typing the address on line 15 from the top at 45 (pica) or at 55 (elite).
   If a printed return address is not used, type the return address on the second line from the top of the envelope and four spaces from the left edge.
2. *Addresses:* The United States Post Office recommends that all addresses be typed in capital letters with no punctuation (see Fig. I-1 and 2).
3. *Zip Codes:* The city, state, and Zip Code are typed on the same line.
   Use the two-letter state abbreviations only if you use the Zip Code. (Fig. I-6 lists the two letter abbreviations.)
   Type the Zip Code two spaces after the state.
4. Attention lines are typed as the second line of the envelope address (see Fig. I-3).
5. Other special notations are illustrated in Figures I-4 and 5.
6. Keep the bottom one-half inch of the envelope free of all typing.

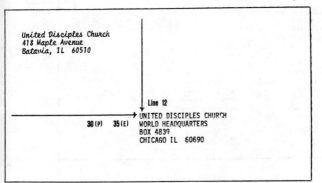

Figure I-1. No. 6¾ envelope

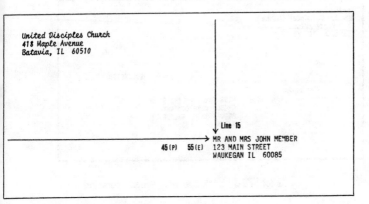

Figure I-2. No. 10 envelope

United Disciples Church
418 Maple Avenue
Batavia, IL 60510

                    CHURCH SUPPLIES INC
                    ATTENTION MARKETING
                    4900 MAPLE AVENUE
                    GENEVA IL 60134

Figure I-3. Envelope with attention line

United Disciples Church
418 Maple Avenue
Batavia, IL 60510

                                        REGISTERED MAIL

                    MISS JANET VOORHEIS
                    CHURCH LIFE COMPANY
                    8000 RAINIER AVENUE
                    AKRON OH 44321

Figure I-4. Envelope with special notation

United Disciples Church
418 Maple Avenue
Batavia, IL 60510

PERSONAL

                    REV JOHN CLARKE
                    FIRST DISCIPLES CHURCH
                    5765 OAK AVENUE
                    STOCKDALE TX 78160

Figure I-5. Envelope with special notation

State	Standard Abbreviation	Two-letter Abbreviation	State	Standard Abbreviation	Two-letter Abbreviation
Alabama	Ala.	AL	Montana	Mont.	MT
Alaska		AK	Nebraska	Nebr.	NE
Arizona	Ariz.	AZ	Nevada	Nev.	NV
Arkansas	Ark.	AR	New Hampshire	N.H.	NH
California	Calif.	CA	New Jersey	N.J.	NJ
Colorado	Colo.	CO	New Mexico	N. Mex.	NM
Connecticut	Conn.	CT	New York	N.Y.	NY
Delaware	Del.	DE	North Carolina	N.C.	NC
Florida	Fla.	FL	North Dakota	N. Dak.	ND
Georgia	Ga.	GA	Ohio		OH
Hawaii		HI	Oklahoma	Okla.	OK
Idaho		ID	Oregon	Oreg.	OR
Illinois	Ill.	IL	Pennsylvania	Pa.	PA
Indiana	Ind.	IN	Rhode Island	R.I.	RI
Iowa		IA	South Carolina	S.C.	SC
Kansas	Kans.	KS	South Dakota	S. Dak.	SD
Kentucky	Ky.	KY	Tennessee	Tenn.	TN
Louisiana	La.	LA	Texas	Tex.	TX
Maine		ME	Utah		UT
Maryland	Md.	MD	Vermont	Vt.	VT
Massachusetts	Mass.	MA	Virginia	Va.	VA
Michigan	Mich.	MI	Washington	Wash.	WA
Minnesota	Minn.	MN	West Virginia	W. Va.	WV
Mississippi	Miss.	MS	Wisconsin	Wis.	WI
Missouri	Mo.	MO	Wyoming	Wyo.	WY

Note: The two-letter abbreviation should always be used on the envelope with the Zip Code. Whether you use it on the inside address of the letter is a matter of personal preference.

Figure I-6.

COPIES

Carbon paper. Carbon paper is available in weights ranging from four to ten pounds per ream. The choice is determined by the number of copies you usually prepare. If you are unfamiliar with carbon paper, talk with your local stationer, who can recommend both the proper carbon and copy paper for your particular needs.

Photocopies. In many offices today the carbon copy has been all but eliminated by the purchase of a copy machine. While photocopies are slightly more expensive than carbon copies, the time saved and convenience of use usually are worth the difference.

Copy machines offer many special features, from collating to reducing original copy to making transparencies. Of course, the cost also increases with the addition of features. However, the least expensive may not be the best for your purposes. The time you spend with a knowledgeable sales representative learning about the various features that are available is well spent.

As was discussed regarding your typewriter, you are the major operator of the copy machine. You should be a part of the selection process. Above all, do not purchase any copy machine that you cannot use in your own office, with no obligation, for a trial period. Experiment with the special features to determine if they are really as easy to use as claimed. Compare the cost of supplies for each machine considered.

In addition to ascertaining that a particular machine can meet your unique needs, consider the following:

1. Is the background of the copy as white as that of the original?
2. Is the copy relatively free of spots, specks, and streaks?

3. Can the machine be adjusted to compensate for a light original?
4. Can the machine be adjusted for, or will it copy, pencil or ink originals?
5. Can copy be run on colored paper?
6. Are you under- or over-buying? In other words, do you have all of the features you need to facilitate your usual processes? Or are you purchasing "nice to have" rather than necessary features?

DUPLICATORS

The two most frequently used duplicators in the church office are stencil and fluid. A few churches now have offset equipment, but this is generally run by someone other than the secretary.

Stencil. Stencil (or ink) duplicators produce up to 3,000 copies from a single stencil and are relatively inexpensive to operate. Special, form-topped stencils can be purchased for typing church bulletins, a feature which can save the secretary a considerable amount of time. Each brand of stencil carries its own directions; a careful reading and following of these should assure very good results.

Electronic stencil makers are enjoying increasing popularity in church offices because the copy is prepared and corrected just as any other original. Photos, cutouts, and similar items can be easily reproduced. More copies can be obtained from a single electronic stencil than from the standard type. Electronic stencils are slightly more expensive, but the ease of preparation and correction is an important factor to many secretaries.

While each secretary who must type many stencils develops her own "tricks of the trade," some of the basic guidelines for achieving optimal results bear repeating. These are:

1. Keep the typewriter keys clean, especially those letters with "open" areas.
2. Set the ribbon lever in the stencil, sometimes white or "off," position.
3. Move the rollers so they do not roll on the stencil surface.
4. When typing lengthwise on a stencil and using a typewriter on which the carriage is not wide enough to accommodate the length, cut only the backing sheet, never the stencil. Merely fold the extra stencil length around the backing sheet for insertion into the typewriter.
5. Experiment to determine the correct key pressure to achieve even cutting of copy.
6. Proof the copy at the end of each paragraph to eliminate unnecessary rolling back of the stencil, thus lessening the chance of tearing it.

Fluid. The fluid (or spirit) duplicator is the least expensive duplicating process and is generally used only for materials to be used within the organization, i.e., working copies for committees, Sunday school worksheets. It should not be used for duplicating the bulletin or other materials for general distribution.

A maximum of 300 copies can be run from a single master. Colored masters are available.

Which process to use? Since cost is always a factor in the church office, the church secretary needs some knowledge of relative costs in order to decide which process to use on a particular job. While any one sales representative will say, with great conviction, that the product being discussed is truly the best for all applications, the following chart may be helpful to you.

No. of Copies	Copy Method	Advantages
1-10	Copier	Fastest Most convenient Least expensive
100+	Duplicator	Fastest Least expensive

11-99	"gray area"
	
	To be determined by
	   time available
	   and usage of copy	

Suggested:
Outside church distribution: copier
Inside church distribution: duplicator

No cost estimates were included in the above chart because these change so rapidly. A good sales representative can supply you with the current cost factors.

6
THE PASTOR'S TOOLS

BUSINESS CARDS

Too often it is thought that the pastor of only a *large* church needs business or calling cards. However, the occasions on which any pastor can use such a card are many: for hospital visitation (especially when the patient is asleep); for identification when calling on new or prospective members; for exchange with colleagues with whom he might wish to correspond; for drop off at community businesses, just to name a few. The calling card represents a small investment in a potentially valuable public relations endeavor.

The card itself should be simply attractive. It should be considered the personal calling card of the pastor, not an announcement of church services. If the church has more than one pastor, the design should be the same with only the name varied. If the church has a logo, it can be placed very discreetly on the card. Likewise, a Scripture reference might be used. A sample card is shown here:

```
┌─────────────────────────────────────────────────┐
│            United Disciples Church              │
│                100 Main Street                  │
│             Anytown, State 00000                │
│                                                 │
│                                                 │
│           I. M. GOODWILL, TH. D.                │
│                    Pastor                       │
│                                                 │
│                                                 │
│ Office: 459-6400              Home: 273-4571    │
└─────────────────────────────────────────────────┘
```

Figure II-1.

A way of making the calling card distinctive without resorting to gimmickry is to change the direction, as illustrated here:

```
┌───────────────────────────┐
│  United Disciples Church  │
│  100 Main Street          │
│  Anytown, State 00000     │
│                           │
│                           │
│                           │
│  I. M. GOODWILL, TH. D.   │
│  Pastor                   │
│                           │
│                           │
│                           │
│  Office: 459-6400         │
│  Home:   273-4571         │
└───────────────────────────┘
```

Figure II-2.

If the pastor wishes to have the calling card provide more information, then a folded card is appropriate (see Fig. II-3). The front of the card will still have the clean appearance of Figure II-1. Announcements of worship services or other desired information should be placed on the inside as shown here.

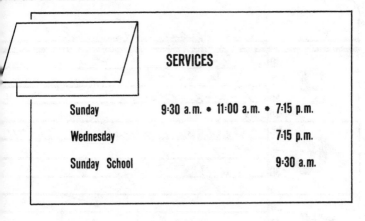

SERVICES

Sunday	9:30 a.m. • 11:00 a.m. • 7:15 p.m.
Wednesday	7:15 p.m.
Sunday School	9:30 a.m.

Figure II-3.

THE PASTOR'S APPOINTMENT BOOK

The pastor's appointment book is his lifeline. Absolute accuracy is demanded. Chapter 4 presents some general tips for maintaining both yours and the pastor's appointment books. Two additional suggestions are:

1. Develop a system for indicating canceled appointments. You may "white out" these and write any changes in the same time slot. Or you may prefer to draw a single line through cancellations, thus preserving a record of all appointments originally scheduled.
2. Consider color coding to indicate the nature of the appointment. For example:
Red: Church business
Blue: Counseling

Black: Personal business and study time
Green: Out-of-town time

A portion of a page in your appointment book might look like this:

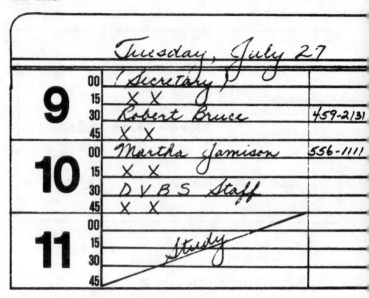

Figure II-4. Portion of page from appointment book

THE PASTOR'S EXPENSES

The one area in which every church needs to take all possible steps to avoid criticism is that of finances. No church is too small to systematize the manner in which funds are paid out. The incidence of the pastor calling the treasurer, reporting that a specified amount was spent, and receiving a check in return, should be very limited.

If your office does not have a form for this purpose, you can design and duplicate your own. If properly designed for your particular needs, the form can be used not only by the pastor but by any other person requesting reimbursement. This can also include the petty cash fund.

A sample form, which you can adapt to your own requirements, is shown as Figure II-5.

No. ____

REQUEST FOR REIMBURSEMENT

To: _____

From: _____

Date: _____

Amount requested: _____

Purpose (attach receipt, if possible)

_____

_____

Requested by _____

Date _____

Approved ____ Date paid _____

Figure II-5.

7
CORRESPONDENCE

The quality of the correspondence that is mailed from your office is a direct reflection upon you and your church. Inconsistent letter styles, uncorrected errors, obvious corrections, outdated or unclear wording—all of these tell the reader that you are either careless or unaware of proper procedures. That may seem to be a harsh judgment; but so often the effect of a very important and well-meant message is diminished, or even lost, by careless preparation.

This same standard of quality applies equally to work done by volunteers. "A volunteer did that" is no excuse for accepting less than the best. Remember Harry Truman's famous "buck"? You, as secretary, are ultimately responsible for every piece of work. You must proof and approve everything that leaves your office. Assume nothing!

LETTERS
This section includes a basic review of letter parts and styles. In addition, specific refinements that should be considered when typing correspondence are checked for your attention.

Figures III-1 and 2 illustrate the two most frequently used letter styles. Figure III-3 highlights each of the letter parts discussed in the succeeding paragraphs.

I. M. Goodwill, Th.D.   Telephone: 123-4567

                         January 1, 1981

    Mr. and Mrs. U. R. Members
    4935 Church Lane
    Oak Park, IL 60303

    Dear Mr. and Mrs. Members:

    This is a sample of a letter typed on full-size stationery in
    modified block style with standard punctuation. This is the
    most frequently used letter style; it conveys an image of con-
    servatism and dependability.

    The date and closing lines begin at the center of the paper.
    The date may also be centered. A colon follows the salutation;
    and a comma, the complimentary close. The paragraphs may or
    may not be indented, depending on the writer's preference.

    The date is typed 2 to 6 lines below the letterhead. This
    placement varies with the length of the letter. The inside
    address begins three lines below the date. There is a double
    space before and after the salutation, between paragraphs, and
    before the complimentary close. The body of the letter is
    single spaced.

    The writer's name is typed on the fourth line below the closing.
    The typist's initials are typed at the left margin a double
    space below the writer's name. The writer's initials are not
    typed.

                         In His service,

                         I. M. Goodwill
                         Pastor

    xxx

Figure III-1. Modified block style/standard punctuation

UNITED DISCIPLES CHURCH

100 Main Street

Anytown, State 00000

I. M. Goodwill, Th.D.
January 1, 1981   Telephone: 123-4567

Mr. and Mrs. U. R. Members
4935 Church Lane
Oak Park, IL 60303

Dear Mr. and Mrs. Members

This is a sample of a letter typed on half-size
stationery in block style. Its features include
all lines beginning at the left margin, no paragraph indentions, 3/4-inch side margins, and open
punctuation.

Since block style projects a progressive image,
many churches prefer the more traditional modified block style. However, a block letter is
the most efficient style since it is not necessary to set any tab stops.

The style you use may also be determined by how
it adds to the balanced appearance of your letter.
Compare the letters in Figures III-1 and 2, and
you will note this balance feature.

This size stationery should be a part of your supplies, along with small envelopes, and should be
used for all short letters.

In His service

I. M. Goodwill
Pastor

xxx

Figure III-2 Block letter/open punctuation

(1) UNITED DISCIPLES CHURCH

100 Main Street

Anytown, State 00000

I. M. Goodwill, Th.D.   Telephone: 123-4567

(2) November 30, 1981

(3) SPECIAL DELIVERY

(4) Midwest Candy Suppliers
179 Congress Avenue
Des Moines, IA 50318

(5) Attention: Shipping Department

(6) Gentlemen

(7) Subject: Christmas Candy Boxes

Our order No. 25 for 1,000 lbs. of assorted candies and 1,500 Christ-max boxes arrived today. However, the shipment actually contained only 750 boxes, as the enclosed billing statement will show.

(8) A staff of volunteers is prepared to pack these boxes on December 5 for distribution on December 15.

Would you please ship the remaining 500 boxes by air immediately.

Best wishes for a happy and blessed Christmas season.

(9) Sincerely

(10) UNITED DISCIPLES CHURCH

(11) Melissa Denna
Director, Christian Education

(12) abc

(13) Enc.

(14) pc Dr. Goodwill

(15) If for any reason you are not able to complete this shipment immediately, please call us on receipt of this letter.

Figure III-3. Letter parts

Letter parts
DATE

1. Always type the date in full on regular correspondence.

May 5, 1929   June 15, 1977

2. Leave 2 to 6 lines between the date and the letterhead. The number of lines is determined by the length of the letter.

MAILING NOTATION

1. Special mailing instructions, such as Special Delivery, Registered Mail, etc., are typed in all caps a double space below the date at the left margin.

INSIDE ADDRESS

1. The inside address is typed, single spaced, at the left margin, usually three spaces below the date.
2. If the recipient of the letter has a title, the title may be typed either following the person's name or on the next line, depending on which placement will result in the most balanced appearance.

Ms. Lila Macy, Manager   Mr. Wallace McIlmurray
Christian Books, Inc.   Regional Sales Director
One Beacon Square   Joy Recordings, Inc.
Fitchburg, MA 01420   South Building, Suite 41
                                Nashville, TN 37202

Do not use redundant titles, such as *Dr.* Marcus Ashley, *Th.D.*

Dr. Marcus Ashley   Marcus Ashley, Th.D.

Reverend is written out only when preceded by *The.*

The Reverend James Kovak   Rev. James Kovak

3. Numbered street names under ten are spelled out.

185 Sixth Street   432 - 59th Street

4. Ordinal endings (-st, -th, -d) are used when the num-

bered street immediately follows the street number. If the street number and name are interrupted by a direction, it is typed without the ordinal ending. Directions are always typed out.

432 West 59 Street

5. Building and house numbers appear as figures with the exception of "one."

One Mayfield Avenue   23 Curtis Avenue

6. The city, state, and Zip Code are typed on the same line. While it is preferable to use the two-letter state abbreviation, it is not incorrect to use the complete name. The standard abbreviations are no longer used. The two-letter state abbreviation is always used on the envelope along with the Zip Code.

ATTENTION LINE

1. The attention line is typed a double space below the inside address at the left margin.

Woodridge Baptist Church
600 West Dravus
Easton, NY 13334

Attention: Director of Missions

SALUTATION

1. The salutation is typed a double space below the inside address—or the attention line when one is used. It is typed at the left margin.
2. The salutation is determined by the first line of the inside address—never by the attention line.

Christian Women Association
Box 1400
Tulsa, OK 74101

Attention: Mary E. Phillips

Mesdames:

3. A semicolon follows the salutation when standard punctuation is used; no punctuation follows when open punctuation is used. A comma following the salutation is not used in business correspondence.

Salutations vary from informal to formal:

Informal	*Dear Dave*
	Dear Janet
Standard salutation	*Dear Mr. Pososki*
	Dear Ms. Harris
Salutation to two men	*Dear Mr. Carlson and Mr. Metz*
	Dear Messrs. Hale and Frye
	Gentlemen
Salutation to two women	*Dear Ms. Keene and Mrs. Hickman*
	Dear Mesdames Howe and Laing
	Mesdames or *Ladies*
Salutation to a group composed of men or of men and women	*Gentlemen*
	Ladies and Gentlemen
Salutation for religious dignitaries	*Dear Rev. Thompson*
	Dear Bishop Mains
	Sir
	Reverend Sir
	Your Eminence

Dear Sirs is an outdated expression and is no longer used.

SUBJECT LINE

1. The subject line is typed a double space below the salutation. If the letter is typed in block style, the subject line begins at the left margin.

Ladies:

Subject: Printing of Missionary Newsletter

2. If the letter is modified block style, the subject line may begin at the left margin, may be centered, or may begin at the paragraph point.

Dear Doctor Hess:

INTRODUCTION OF VIDEO MINISTRY

Dear Major Andrews:

Christmas Collection Permit

3. The word *Subject* may appear, but there is a tendency to omit it. *Re* or *In Re* is generally reserved for insurance companies, financial institutions, legal offices, and government agencies.
4. Type the subject line in all caps or underline it. When an attention line is also used, match the form of the two lines.

Attention: Marta E. Goebel

Ladies:

Annual Report

BODY

1. The body begins a double space below the salutation— or below the subject line when one is used.
2. The contents of the letter are single spaced with double spacing between paragraphs.

Dear Rev. Moore:

Many fond memories came to mind when I received your invitation to speak at Camp Muckaluck.

It would be my privilege to serve as guest pastor during the week of July 5.

3. The paragraphs are never indented in block style letters.

4. The paragraphs in modified block style letters may or may not be indented, depending on the writer's preference.

5. When a letter requires two or more pages, succeeding pages are typed on plain stationery of the same quality and color as the letterhead.

   Each succeeding page carries a heading for identification purposes. Either of the following forms are correct, although the first one shown is most frequently used with block style correspondence.

   Mrs. Kathy Kittle
   Page 2
   July 27, 1981

   Mrs. Kathy Kittle   2   July 27, 1981

   (The second heading shown begins and ends with the left and right margins.)

6. The heading is typed one inch from the top of the page. A triple space separates the heading and the body of the letter.

COMPLIMENTARY CLOSE

1. Type the complimentary close a double space below the body. Its placement depends on the letter style used (review Fig. III-1 and 2). Only the first word of the complimentary close is capitalized.

2. If standard punctuation is used, a comma follows the complimentary close. If open punctuation is used, no punctuation follows it.

3. The tone of the complimentary close should match the salutation. Thus, a more formal salutation requires a formal complimentary close.

   Typical complimentary closes, arranged in groups from informal to formal, are:

Cordially	Yours truly
Cordially yours	Yours very truly
Yours cordially	Very truly yours

Sincerely	Yours respectfully
Sincerely yours	Respectfully
Yours sincerely	

Along with the trend toward making letters more conversational, there is a tendency to select those closings that do not include "Yours."

4. Many pastors prefer to use a personal closing with religious overtones. This is a matter of personal preference and can, indeed, add warmth and sincerity to the tone of the letter.

| In His love | In Christian service |
| In His service | In Christian love |

With Christ's blessings

CHURCH NAME

1. Some churches still prefer to repeat the name of the church a double space below the complimentary close. Since it already appears in the letterhead, this is unnecessary but not incorrect.

With Christian concern,

UNITED DISCIPLES CHURCH

I. M. Goodwill, Pastor

SIGNATURE LINE

1. The writer's name is usually typed four lines below the complimentary close or the church name, if used. More or fewer lines may be left if necessary to achieve a balanced appearance.

2. If the writer's title follows the name, a comma precedes it. If the writer's title is typed on the next line, no punctuation is used.

| I. M. Goodwill, Pastor | I. M. Goodwill |
| | Pastor |

3. Personal titles of men, such as *Mr.*, and professional

titles of men and women, such as *Rev., Dr.,* are not included in the signature lines, even in parentheses.

4. A woman who wishes to designate her marital status may include the appropriate title in parentheses before her name.

(Ms.) Abigail Madison   (Mrs.) Gina LaFollette

5. When the church secretary writes a letter for someone else, the signature line appears as follows:

Jeanette Caldwell
Secretary to Douglas Thompson

REFERENCE INITIALS

1. The reference initials of the typist are typed in lower case at the left margin a double space below the last line of the signature lines.

Sincerely

R. D. Springfield
District Superintendent

pes

2. The dictator's initials may be used, but there is a tendency to omit these since the complete name appears in the signature lines. Sample reference initials are:

srp   JDarren/srp
JMS/srp
JMS:srp

ENCLOSURE NOTATION

1. The enclosure notation serves two purposes: (a) To remind the typist to enclose something mentioned in the letter, and (b) to remind the addressee to check to see that the enclosure is included.

The enclosure notation is typed a double space below the reference initials. Like reference initials, it may assume a variety of styles:

Enclosure	Enclosures
Enc.	Encls.

2. If more than one item is enclosed, the number should be indicated.

Enclosures 3

3. If an item of value is enclosed, the item should be named.

Enc. check	Enc. 2 certificates

COPY NOTATION

1. The copy notation is used when the correspondence is also being sent to persons other than the addressee. It is typed a double space below the reference initials or enclosure notation, when used. It is typed at the left margin.
2. The form of the notation is determined by the type of copy:

   cc is used strictly for carbon copies.

   pc is limited to photocopies.

   Copy or *c* may be used for either.
3. The names of the recipients are ranked by importance when appropriate; otherwise, they are alphabetized.

cc Loren Randall, Bishop
Craig Cox, Superintendent
Hernando Lopez, Coordinator

pc Althea Brandel
Christina Childers
Tina McKay

POSTSCRIPT

1. The postscript is the last item in a letter and is typed a double space below the copy notation. Like the paragraphs in the letter, it is single spaced.
2. The postscript should be used sparingly. Either of the following forms is correct.

cc L. Lane

P.S. Don't forget the Area Planning Council meeting on July 10 at the Bridgeport church.

pc

Rev. Jackson called this morning to report that the issue you raised will be added to next week's agenda. See you then!

Forms of address. Since forms of address for other professional persons are a part of nearly every other secretarial handbook, only those for the clergy are included in Figure III-4.

Your church or denomination may have developed unique forms of address consistent with its own practices.

An example is the custom of many congregations of addressing each other as "Brother" and "Sister." If that is typical of your church, your pastor may wish to use those as salutations in correspondence. The resulting inside address and salutation would then appear as:

Mr. Andrew Atchinson
26 Shady Lane
Boxwell, OK 74727

Dear Brother Atchinson:

Such a practice would not be considered a violation of the rule of consistency of first line of inside address and salutation.

NEWS RELEASE

Most churches list schedules of worship services in the local newspaper. Fewer churches take full advantage of the news release to create and build interest in the church and its activities. As church secretary, you can be responsible for obtaining excellent free publicity by knowing how to type complete and accurate news releases. Included here are tips for "getting published."

FORMS OF ADDRESS

Clergy	Letter Address	Salutation	Closing
Protestant Clergy			
Bishop (Episcopalian)	The Right Reverend —— Bishop of —— (Address)	Right Reverend Sir: Right Reverend and Dear Sir:	Respectfully yours,
		My dear Bishop —: Dear Bishop —:	Sincerely yours, Sincerely,
	or The Very Reverend —— Dean of —— (Address)	Very Reverend Sir: Dear Dean —:	Respectfully yours, Sincerely,
Bishop (Methodist, Protestant)	The Reverend ——, D.D.[1]	Reverend Sir: Dear Sir: My dear Bishop —: Dear Bishop —:	Respectfully yours, Sincerely yours, Sincerely, Sincerely yours,
Minister	The Reverend —— *or* The Reverend ——, D.D.	Dear Sir: Reverend Sir: Dear Reverend: Dear Mr. (or Doctor[2]):	Sincerely yours,
Jewish Clergy			
Rabbi	Rabbi —— (Address)	Dear Rabbi —:	Sincerely,
Chaplains			
	Chaplain —— (rank and service designation) (Address)	Dear Chaplain —:	Sincerely,

Catholic Clergy

Cardinal	His Eminence ―― Cardinal ―― Archbishop of ―― (Address)	Your Eminence: Dear Cardinal ――:	Respectfully yours, Sincerely,
Archbishop/Bishop	The Most Reverend ―――― Archbishop of ―― *or* Bishop of ―― (Address)	Your Excellency: Dear Archbishop ――: Dear Bishop ――:	Respectfully yours, Sincerely,
Monsignor	The Very Reverend Monsignor ―― (Address)	Very Reverend Monsignor: Dear Monsignor:	Respectfully yours, Sincerely,
Priest	The Reverend ―― (add initials of order) (Address)	Reverend Sir: Dear Father ――:	Respectfully yours, Sincerely,
Sister	Sister ――(add initials of order) (Address)	Dear Sister: Dear Sister ――:	Sincerely,

Figure III-4.

[1] A title and a degree may both be used.
[2] *Doctor* is written out when only the surname is used.

1. Always check with your local newspaper editors to learn of any format preferences they may have for news releases. Most important, observe those preferences.

2. Enhance the possibility of your news being printed by developing a working relationship with the editor of church news for your paper. That person might be a specialist in religious news or might be a multipurpose editor. In either case, know him or her. Then, mail releases directly to that person.

3. Remember that a news release is unsolicited news and, therefore, must be newsworthy.

4. Since it is unlikely that your church has a printed form for news releases, a simple format for you to follow is shown as Figure III-5. Typing guidelines for news releases are:

   a. Even though you may choose to vary the style as shown here, you must include all of the information in the heading. Each item is necessary.

   b. Always give the article a title, even if it is always changed by the editor.

   c. Leave wide margins for the editor's use. Double space the text.

   d. Confine the release to one page if possible. If more than one page is necessary, type "more" on the bottom of each page.

   e. Type # # # at the end of the release.

   f. Editors cut from the bottom up, so be sure that all vital information is contained in the first few sentences.

POSTAL SERVICES

Have you ever thought that once you deposited the day's mail in the mailbox your responsibility for it was over? That, however, can only be assumed if you are sure that

United Disciples Church
100 Main Street
Anytown, State 00000

N E W S   R E L E A S E

To: San Valley Times

For Release: IMMEDIATELY

Contact: Barbara Oldford

CRISIS PHONE INSTALLED

435-7968 or H-E-L-P Y-O-U is the new number of a crisis phoneline now in operation at United Disciples Church. Any person of any age experiencing a crisis is urged to call immediately. Trained Counselors answer the telephone 24 hours each day.

The HELP YOU line is one more evidence of the commitment of United Disciples Church to extend the love of Christ into the community. Its installation follows the very successful WHEELS of last year, a mobile meals program for shut-in senior citizens, and the earlier HAPPY TRAILS, a camping program for handicapped youngsters.

If you would like to know more about this exciting program and the part you can play in it, call the church office (435-1000) between 9 a.m. and 5 p.m.

# # #

Figure III-5.

each item was properly prepared for efficient handling and was mailed in the most expeditious manner. That is also why it is so important that the church secretary have adequate information about available postal services.

The charts that follow (Fig. III-6 and 7) summarize the classes of mail and describe the special services. In addition, the United States Postal Service publishes brochures regularly with the latest information on postal services. Copies can be obtained from your local post office or by writing to:

> The Consumer Advocate
> U. S. Postal Service
> Washington, DC 20260

Postage meters. Many secretaries, even those who handle a relatively small volume of mail, have found that the nominal cost of a postage meter is more than offset by the convenience. Some of its advantages are:

1. Eliminates the need for purchasing and keeping stamps of various denominations.
2. Controls and records the amount of postage used.
3. Prints directly onto envelopes and also provides a tape for packages.
4. Expedites the handling of mail at the post office.

The meter is taken to the post office periodically where postage is paid for in advance. See your postmaster for more information.

LETTER SAMPLES

On the following pages are the message portions of letters that are frequently prepared in the church office.

While you may be able to use some of these letters just

Class	Content Description	Rates Special Instructions	Limitations
First Class	All handwritten and typewritten messages Postal cards Checks Statements of account Business Reply Mail	Rate determined per ounce Mail not letter size: Mark "First Class"	Up to 12 ounces
Priority Mail	First class mail over 12 ounces	Rate determined by weight and distance Mark "Priority Mail"	Maximum: 70 lbs. 100 in.: length and girth combined
Second Class	Newspapers Magazines	Contact post office for specific requirements	
Third Class	Advertising mail	Two rate classes: single piece and bulk rate	Maximum: 16 oz.
Fourth Class (Parcel Post)	Packages	Rate determined by weight and distance Library rate available for certain items	Over 16 oz.

MINIMUM SIZE STANDARDS FOR ALL MAIL: Must be at least .007 thick (approximately that of a postcard)
Must be at least 3½ inches in height and 5 inches in length
Must be rectangular

Figure III-6

SPECIAL MAIL SERVICES

Service	Description
Special Delivery	Provides for delivery during certain hours beyond delivery of normal mail. Available for all classes of mail, but not all post offices have special delivery service.
Express Mail	Overnight delivery service. Not available at all post offices.
PROOF OF MAILING AND DELIVERY:	
Certificate of Mailing	Serves only as proof of mailing. Does not guarantee or prove delivery. Nominal cost.
Certified Mail	Provides a mailing receipt and a record of delivery at destination post office. Designed for items of no intrinsic value. Return receipt (proof of delivery): additional fee.
Return Receipt	Available for insured mail under $15. Available for certified, registered, and COD mail.
Restricted Delivery	Delivery made only to addressee.
MAILING OF VALUABLES:	
Insurance	Available up to $400 for third class, parcel post mail and for first-class merchandise.
Registered Mail	Should be used for all irreplaceable mail. Provides insurance up to $25,000. Return receipt: additional fee.
COD	Amount of merchandise, plus postage and COD fee, collected from addressee. Available for first class, third class, and parcel post. Limited to $400.

Figure III-7

as they are written, it is assumed that the greater use will be as "models" for church correspondence and that you will add to, delete from, and modify them to make them uniquely yours.

The sample messages are in five categories:

> The church family
> Information requests
> Membership
> Visitors
> General

The church family. Letters sent to members on personal occasions need not be lengthy, but they must be sincere. The important thing is that the church cared enough to write!

The first letter begins with a verse of Scripture. It is possible to add this to any type of letter and is a quietly beautiful witness.

Bereavement

. . . for the Lord hath comforted his people . . . (Isaiah 49:13).

The family of United Disciples Church echoes the words of the prophet in extending sympathy to you and your family during this time of bereavement.

It is the prayer of each of us that you will truly know the comfort that only God can provide.

In Christian love,

Congratulations

Congratulations on your *(graduation, promotion, new baby, etc.)*

Each member of your church family shares in the joy of this happy occasion.

May God's continued rich blessings be yours.

With warm regards,

Stewardship

Enclosed is your financial statement for _____. Thank you for sharing this portion of that which God has given you.

Truly we at United Disciples Church labor together in meeting the needs of His kingdom. It is exciting to see just how wonderfully God works through the commitment of people and resources.

Again, thank you for your faithful support.

In appreciation,

As you know, we at United Disciples Church have been experiencing a shortage of finances for several weeks.

It is difficult for me to write this letter because each of you has been so faithful in your support. However, I feel I must ask you to reexamine your current level of giving. Could you possibly increase that level to help us during the next month?

A series of budget cuts and revisions have been put into effect, so you may rest assured that we are also good stewards of God's money. We believe that, with an extra boost over the next few weeks, we can return to a sound financial base.

Won't you pray about this matter and ask God how you can help your church during this critical time.

In prayerful concern,

Leadership Roles

We are in the process of naming the members of the _____ Committee for the coming year. This letter is your invitation to serve as a member of that group.

I believe that your talents can be uniquely used in this area. I hope you will give prayerful consideration to accepting this invitation.

I would appreciate knowing your decision by _____ so that our planning for a fruitful year may be completed.

In His service,

You have been nominated for the office of _____ of United Disciples Church. This nomination represents the confidence that fellow members have placed in you.

While election to this office requires a firm commitment on your part, it an honor to be called to be a part of the leadership team of God's church.

Details of the expectations of this office are enclosed for your consideration.

I do not believe that this decision should be made alone. Please discuss with your family. Above all, pray diligently for the mind of the Spirit.

I too will be praying for you during this time of decision.

In His service,

Moreover, it is required in stewards that a man be found faithful (1 Cor. 4:2).

Thank you for serving so faithfully on the _____ Committee during the past _____.

Only as we labor together, can we build the kingdom of God.

Your committed stewardship of time and energy is sincerely appreciated.

In His service,

Expressions of appreciation. Too often the pastor and other members forget to say "thank you" to those persons who labor very faithfully in "lesser" roles—the flower arrangers, the cookie bakers, the lawn mowers, etc. These may be lesser roles in terms of prestige; but these people are using their abilities freely for God's work and thus are great in his sight. It should be a periodic and regular practice of the church office to express appreciation to such persons.

Thank you

May I take this opportunity to thank you for the hours of volunteer work you have contributed to United Disciples Church.

There are many tasks to be done, and it requires many willing hands and hearts if we are to fulfill our mission. The faithfulness of persons like yourself help to make this possible.

Again, thank you very much. May the love of Christ which you have demonstrated be returned to you.

In grateful appreciation,

Thank you! Such a simple expression but how often we forget to say it.
Thank you! Your many hours of faithful service to United Disciples Church are gratefully appreciated.
Thank you! Thank you!

In appreciation,

Just a note to say thank you for the time you spent making our
_____ successful.
It was a beautiful occasion and one to be long remembered.

In appreciation,

Information Requests

Letters requesting or verifying information should be brief and concise. While such letters are always courteous, they need not convey a strong sense of warmth like other letters.

REQUEST FOR INFORMATION

_____ have indicated a desire to join United Disciples Church. Would you please provide the following information:

_____ Baptism _____
(date)
_____ Marriage _____
(date, if applicable)
_____ Membership _____
(date)

Thank you for your assistance.

Sincerely,

Please note that only "thank you . . ." is used, never "thank you in advance. . . ."

VERIFICATION OF INFORMATION

In response to your request of _____, this will verify that
_____ was baptized at United Disciples Church on
_____.

or

_____ were married at United Disciples Church on
_____.

or

_____ joined United Disciples Church on
_____ and are members in good standing.
If you need any additional information, please feel free to contact me.

Sincerely,

In response to your request of _____, I am sorry but I have
been unable to find the information you requested.
If you or _____ could give me an approximate date on
which they (joined, were baptized, were married), I will be happy to
search our records further.

Sincerely,

Membership
MEMBERSHIP CLASSES

We are pleased that you have expressed an interest in membership in
United Disciples Church.
Membership information classes will begin on _____ at
_____. Pastor Goodwill will lead these sessions.
Membership in any body of believers is a matter for careful, prayerful
decision. We will be praying, along with you, for the guidance of the Holy
Spirit as you consider taking this step.

In His service,

INVITATION TO MEMBERSHIP

On behalf of the congregation of United Disciples Church, I want to
thank you for worshiping with us on several occasions recently.
We are wondering whether we can provide any further information
about our church for you at this time. As you know, we offer a full range of
programs for the entire family. Details appear in each Sunday's bulletin.

As also announced in the bulletin, we will be starting a new series of membership information classes on _____ at _____. We invite you to join us in these classes. A commitment to join our church is not necessary. Rather, these session are designed to acquaint you with our church and to explore our common belief in Jesus Christ.

Won't you make plans now to participate in this opportunity to share your faith.

In His love,

NEW MEMBERS

We are pleased that you have completed your membership classes and have decided to join United Disciples Church.

New members will be received on Sunday, _____, at the 9:30 service. The front rows will be reserved for you and your family. A coffee hour will follow the service.

As you know, United Disciples Church is an exciting place to worship. We are grateful when new persons catch a glimpse of the mission of our church and choose to become a part of us.

Welcome to a caring congregation!

With warm regards,

Visitors. (These messages could also be printed on post cards.)

IN-TOWN VISITOR

Thank you for visiting United Disciples Church last Sunday.

We hope you received a warm welcome and will return soon.

If I may answer any questions about our church or be of assistance in any way, please feel free to call me.

In His service,

OUT-OF-TOWN VISITOR

Thank you for visiting United Disciples Church.

We hope that the warmth of our love, as it flows from His love, was felt by you.

Please visit us again whenever you are in our area.

In His service,

General (or miscellaneous)

INVITATION TO SPEAKER

The Evangelism Committee of United Disciples Church has set aside the week of May 5 through 10, 19--, as "Spiritual Growth for Self and Family." We would like to invite you to be the featured speaker for that week.

Specifically, your speaking schedule would be:

Sunday, May 5—Two morning services
           One evening service

May 6-10   —One evening service
           each day

In addition, you would be the guest of the Women's Association at their spring luncheon on May 7 and would be asked to bring greetings to the group. We also have small study groups of varying interests that meet at the church during the week. You might be asked to join one or more of these groups for informal discussion.

We recognize that this is a heavy schedule. We are prepared to compensate you accordingly. More importantly, the commitment to spiritual growth of our members is such that we are also committed to prayer and attendance support.

Won't you give this matter your prayerful consideration. We will look forward to hearing from you in the next two or three weeks.

Sincerely,

RESPONSE TO SPEAKING INVITATIONS

Thank you for your invitation to address the Christian Businesswomen's Association on _____. I am pleased to accept.

I have heard so much about your group that I am looking forward to meeting with you on that date.

(or)

(same first sentence).

I wish I could be with you on that date; but, unfortunately, I have a prior commitment.

Won't you ask me again at some time in the future?

Sincerely,

RESPONSE TO BUILDING USE REQUESTS

Thank you for thinking of United Disciples Church when planning your upcoming meeting.

We are happy to confirm the following arrangements:

Group _____

Date _____

Time _____

Special arrangements/equipment _____

_____

Enclosed are the guidelines for using the church facilities. Please read these carefully and share them with members of your group.

May God truly bless your efforts.

Sincerely,

Thank you for thinking of United Disciples Church when planning your upcoming meeting.

While we do try to cooperate with community groups in many ways, it is a policy of our church that the building and facilities may only be used for church and church-related groups and activities. Therefore, we are unable to grant this request.

We hope you will understand our position. We wish your group much success.

Sincerely,

REQUEST FOR BIDS

United Disciples Church is currently soliciting bids on the following:

(Complete description of job to be done or equipment desired)

The closing date for receiving bids is _____ p.m. on
_____. Bids will be awarded no later than _____.

Sincerely,

REQUEST FOR PRODUCT INFORMATION

United Disciples Church is considering the possibility of purchasing

_____.

Would you please send us complete information on your product line.

We would appreciate it if any calls to our office regarding this inquiry be made on Tuesday mornings directly to my secretary.

Sincerely,

REQUEST FOR ADDRESS UPDATE

The following or similar address update request should be sent to any members for whom you do not have a current address. If you type "Address Correction Requested" on the envelope, the post office will forward the letter and return a form showing the new address to your office. The fee for this is very nominal.

The address information we have in our files for you is apparently incorrect. As you know, it is my desire to maintain close relations with all members of the UDC family.

Therefore, would you please assist us by sending or calling in your new address and telephone number to the church office. In fact, why not do it while you are thinking about it.

If I may be of any assistance to you or your family, please call me.

In Christian love,

8
INTERNAL COMMUNICATIONS

While external communications of the church office are important because the impression they convey is often that of "The Church," a totally smooth functioning of your office on a day-to-day basis is often determined largely by the processes you use for internal communications. This section should prove useful as it reviews the forms that are so important to that process—memorandums, message forms, work and building requests, inventories, and the pesky, but necessary, petty cash voucher.

MEMORANDUMS

Written internal communications are transmitted through the use of memorandums. Memorandums are not prepared for distribution outside the church.

If you type memos frequently, you should order a supply of printed forms, both full and half sheets. Consider the possibility of carbonless forms to save time in preparing copies. A sample memo form is shown as Figure IV-1. When ordering printed forms, be certain that the spacing of the guide words aligns with standard typewriter spacing.

If your typing of memorandums is less frequent, you can prepare your own forms very easily. Following are guidelines both for the preparation of the memo form and for typing memos.

1. Memos may be either on full or half sheets of plain paper, depending on the length of the message.
2. To prepare a memo form, type MEMORANDUM in all capitals, one inch from the top of the page and one inch from the left edge of the paper. Triple space and type each of the guide words. The guides should be double spaced. Two styles of memo forms are illustrated here.

MEMORANDUM	MEMORANDUM
To:	To:
From:	From:
Date:	Date:
Subject:	Subject:

3. Whichever style you select, align your typing to begin two spaces after the *Subject* guide. Triple space to begin the message.
4. The message also begins one inch from the left edge or in line with the heading. While the message is usually single spaced, short messages may be double spaced.
5. The typist's reference initials are typed a double space below the message. Any appropriate enclosure notation is added a double space below the initials.
6. If the memo is going to more than one person, the

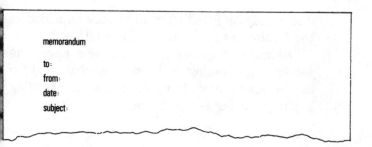

memorandum

to:

from:

date:

subject:

Figure IV-1. Sample memorandum

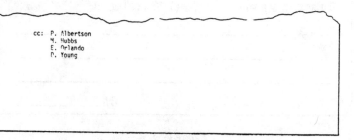

cc: P. Albertson
    M. Hubbs
    E. Orlando
    D. Young

Figure IV-2. Distribution list

names may be listed after *To* or may be added at the bottom, as illustrated in Figure IV-2.

7. If the memo requires more than one page, the second page heading is the same as that used for letters (see page 90). Triple space after the heading before resuming the message.

MESSAGES

Recording messages accurately is one of the most important tasks of the secretary. In the church office where a volunteer may be answering the phone or greeting callers, it is equally important that that person be thoroughly knowledgeable about the message-taking procedures of your office.

```
┌─────────────────────────────────────────────────────┐
│                      MESSAGE                          │
│                                                       │
│  To _____ Date _____        │
│  M _____        │
│  Phone _____ Time _____     │
│  ☐ Telephoned         ☐ Please phone                  │
│  ☐ Returned your call ☐ Wants to see you              │
│  ☐ Came to see you    ☐ Will call again               │
│  Message _____        │
│  _____        │
│  _____        │
│                                      By _____      │
└─────────────────────────────────────────────────────┘
```

Figure IV-3.

A sample message form is shown here to provide a means of reviewing the key items. Similar forms may be purchased very inexpensively at your stationers.

The following points should be observed when taking messages.

1. Every message should be recorded. Never trust your own or anyone else's memory. Too many things can happen between the time the call is received and the time it is transmitted to use memory as the medium.

2. Record all calls on a standard form—not on loose pieces of paper. Purchased forms are usually on colored paper so they are readily indentifiable as messages.

3. Each item on the message form should be completed.

    Incidentally, if a caller has called several times previously or is a member of the church, it should not be necessary for you to ask the spelling of the name. You should know it!

    Also, if two or more members have the same name (for example, my church has three William Reid families), use some type of identifier so the pastor knows which one is calling.

4. Verify the caller's number by repeating it.

5. Recording the time of the call is important. The person being called may have seen or talked with the caller since the message was taken. Thus, knowing the time can help to eliminate unnecessary return calls.

6. Indicate clearly what the caller's wishes are by checking the appropriate category.

7. Repeat the gist of the message, if necessary, to be certain that what you have recorded is accurate.

8. If you handle calls for several persons within the

office, develop a systematic way of transmitting the messages to each person, being certain to maintain confidentiality at all times.

In addition to message forms, some secretaries maintain a telephone log of all incoming calls. This is unusual and should be done only for a reason unique to your office. If you have such a need, a sample log is shown as Figure IV-4.

Priority calls. A "priority call" is defined as a call regarding illness, hospitalization, death, or a crisis of any type. The priority call is routine within the church office and is truly given "priority" in handling.

It is the one type of call that must have followup of an appropriate nature. That followup can assume many forms:

Referral to a pastor
Referral to another church official
Referral to an agency, group, or person qualified to give assistance
Follow through by yourself
Other action appropriate for your situation

All crisis calls should be recorded with action taken indicated. You may use a form similar to Figure IV-4 but use it only for crisis situations; you may prepare a log specifically for these calls as shown as Figure IV-5; or you may design a message form (Figure IV-6) so that you have feedback from appropriate people. This is particularly desirable in larger churches where several different persons may respond to crisis calls, depending on the nature of the call.

TELEPHONE LOG

Date	Time	Caller	Nature of Call	Referred to	Additional Information

Figure IV-4.

ILLNESS/HOSPITAL INFORMATION SHEET

DATE	MEMBER	NATURE OF ILLNESS	LOCATION	CALL REQUEST REFERRED TO	DATE CALL MADE	FOLLOWUP NEEDED
						Yes No

Figure IV-5.

PRIORITY MESSAGE

To _____ Date _____

* * * * *

Caller _____

Location _____

_____

Nature of priority _____

(Surgery scheduled) _____

Pertinent information _____

_____

_____

Date of followup _____
(Please return this form to church office when call has been completed. Thank you.)

. . . comfort ye my people . . . (Isaiah 40:1).

Figure IV-6.

WORK REQUEST FORMS

Unlike secretaries in other types of offices, the church secretary receives her work from many different sources. In the absence of a system, this can be overwhelming. Thus, it is important that the procedures for handling incoming work be established and distributed.

To be successful the system must include two processes: A plan for receiving work and a plan for completing it. A work request form, such as that shown in Figure IV-7, is one of the simplest means of implementing these procedures.

WORK REQUEST

Person requesting work _____

Department _____ Date _____

* * * * *

Date needed _____ No. of copies needed _____

Instructions:

_____

Please list the name and telephone number of the person to be
contacted if questions arise during the preparation of the work.

Name _____ Tel. No. _____

Figure IV-7.

In addition, guidelines should be given whenever persons
request that work be done. These should be simple but
firm. Sample guidelines might include the following:

GUIDELINES FOR WORK
TO BE PREPARED BY THE
CHURCH OFFICE

1. All work to be done must be submitted three days
   prior to its being needed.
2. A work request form (available in the church office) must be attached to all work. Please provide
   clear instructions for preparing and running final
   copies. Unless a specific type of duplicating is
   needed and so indicated, the church secretary will
   determine how to run the copies, based on the
   number needed and the distribution.
3. A contact person must be named in the event that

questions arise during the preparation of the work.

4. The church office staff recognizes that emergencies do occur, and every effort is made to accommodate these. This is most easily accomplished when everyone tries to minimize the number of "rush" jobs.

5. Your office staff is happy to assist you as you fulfill your responsibilities to our Lord and His church. Please do not hestitate to ask for our assistance if you need it.

Figure IV-8.

Work to be done should be placed in a folder, the most recently received on top. Then, by working from the bottom, you assure yourself and everyone else that work is completed in the order received.

BUILDING/ROOM REQUEST FORMS

If you have ever been the target of two persons or groups both adamantly claiming that they "reserved that room long ago," you know just how important it is that all building/room requests be processed in written form.

Since the policies and procedures for using church facilities can and do differ considerably from one church to another, only a suggested form (Figure IV-9) is presented here. This contains the vital information that would be needed in most situations. You may certainly want to modify this form to meet your own facility needs.

One word of caution, particularly applicable to outside groups: If your church has policies and rules for the use of church facilities, be certain that these are conveyed in writing to the responsible person(s) and that, in turn, that person conveys the same to the entire group. Leave nothing to chance. Never assume that people know you "don't do *that* in a church"!

129

UNITED DISCIPLES CHURCH
Building/Room Request

This form must be in the church office five days prior to the requested date.

Group _____ No. of persons attending _____

Person responsible _____

Purpose of meeting _____

_____

Facility requested _____ Date of meeting _____

Time of meeting: Beginning _____ Ending _____

Furniture arrangement: (please draw diagram)

* * * * *

Equipment Requested

    Audiovisual (check all applicable)

        Projector: Movie ___ Slide ___ Overhead ___

        Microphone ___ Lectern ___ Chalkboard ___

    Kitchen*

        Coffee pot ___ Number needed ___

        Dishes ___ Silverware ___ Paper products ___

        Stove ___ Refrigerator ___ Dishwasher ___

*A $5 fee is charged whenever kitchen facilities or equipment are used.

Person making request _____ Date _____

Figure IV-9.

EQUIPMENT INVENTORY

A current equipment inventory is needed by every church. If your church does not have one, begin to prepare one immediately. Set a date for completion because this is one of those jobs on which it is easy to procrastinate. Enlist the help of your maintenance staff, or even volunteers, to inventory each room of the church building. Include all items of value.

Or, if you have an inventory but it is outdated, assume the same urgency for the project and bring it up to date now. Then set definite dates for maintaining it in future months.

The information you need for the inventory includes:

1. Name of item
2. Location (or a separate sheet can be maintained for each room)
3. Manufacturer or source
4. Date of purchase
5. Price

If the church inventory is maintained by someone other than yourself, you will still want to keep an inventory of office equipment. This can be maintained on 3 x 5 cards (Figure IV-10). This record can be a valuable aid whenever service is needed.

Item: _Typewriter_   Location _Ch. Ed._

Date of purchase: _6-15-77_   Price _555 00_

Source: _Machine Sales Inc._   Ser. No. _12-49-753_

Service record: 6-12-78   Cleaning   40 00
              7- 2-79   "   45 00
              5-5-80   Tab sticking   22 00

Figure IV-10.

131

PETTY CASH FUND

Small purchases within the church office, such as postage, supplies, and refreshments, are usually made from the petty cash fund. This fund is typically set up for twenty to twenty five dollars and is maintained by the secretary. It should be kept in a safe place at all times and locked up after hours.

In maintaining the petty cash fund, the secretary completes two forms: a petty cash voucher and a petty cash journal. A petty cash voucher should be completed as soon as any funds are expended because this is an easy item to forget later. The journal is used to prepare a report for the treasurer when the fund needs to be replenished. Both are illustrated here.

PETTY CASH VOUCHER

$ ______________ No. ______

Paid to ______________________________

For ______________________________

____

____

Received by ______________________________
(signature)

Figure IV-11.

1981 Date		Ref.	Debits	Credits	Balance
Jan. 2	Cash		25 —		25 —
3	Office Supplies	101		7 39	17 61
6	Coffee	102		5 75	11 86
14	S.S. pencils	103		3 14	8 72
20	Stamps	104		3 60	5 12
	Balance Fwd. 1-31-81		5 12		5 12
	Received from Treasurer		19 88		25 —

Figure IV-12. Petty cash journal

9
REPORTS

Report typing in the church office assumes many forms — from the informal committee summary to the formal annual report to the congregation and includes such items as agendas, minutes, and financial statements. While it is difficult, if not impossible, to specify formats that would meet the needs of every church, a general review of the more frequently typed reports may be helpful. Hopefully then, these principles can be adapted to your situation.

FORMAT

The first principle of report preparation should be that of consistency. In other words, a report originating in any one of the church offices should look like that coming from any other one. This can be accomplished as you, as church secretary, in cooperation with the total staff, begin to assemble an office style manual for your church. In the large church this manual can serve as a reference point for all secretaries. In the smaller church it can be used by volunteers or by your vacation replacement. In any situation it is an invaluable source for new employees.

General principles of report typing are shown as Figures V-I and V-II. More specific formats for particular reports follow.

1. A one-inch (seven lines) top margin is a minimum standard for informal reports.
2. A two-inch (thirteen lines) top margin is used on the first page of a formal report.
3. Side and bottom margins are one inch.
4. If the report is to be placed in a binder or folder, use a one-and-a-half inch left margin. All other margins remain one inch.

   If a one-and-a-half-inch left margin is used, shift the centering point three spaces to the right.
5. Center the title in all caps on line thirteen from the top. Triple space before beginning the body.
6. Double spacing is preferable for reports. However, if space is limited, single spacing may be used with double spacing between paragraphs.

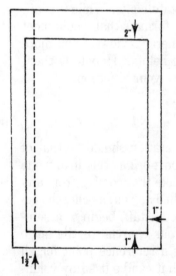

Figure V-1.
First page of a report

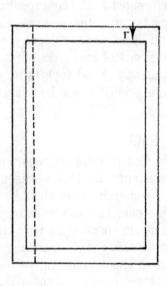

Figure V-2.
Succeeding page of a report

Headings. Figure V-3 illustrates the placement of headings within a report.

Page 3

Board of Deacons

The Board of Deacons reported a total of 1,452 member contacts during the past year—a net increase of 12 percent. Other extensions of the diaconal ministry occurred in the Good Shepherd and Good Samaritan programs.
Good Shepherds. As the spiritual shepherds of the UDC family, six new

Figure V-3. Headings in a report

Pagination. Note the placement of the page number in Figure V-3. It is typed on line 4 from the top of the page ending at the right margin. It may also be typed one-half inch from the bottom of the page. However, this is a more difficult position in which to achieve consistency. The first page of a report is generally not numbered.

AGENDAS

Two types of agendas are illustrated in this section—informal and formal.

First, the informal agenda (Figure V-4) is simply a list of topics to be covered in a particular meeting. If possible, the list should be arranged in order of importance. Then, if time runs out, the remaining items can constitute the beginnings of the agenda for the next meeting.

The informal agenda should be considered a necessary tool for any meeting, regardless of the number of persons involved. Since many church meetings do not adhere to strict parliamentary procedure, particularly when only a few persons are involved, planning ahead is also often neglected. Much valuable time is lost without a structure.

AGENDA
Flower Distribution Committee
April 13, 1980

1. Introduction of members of committee
2. Statement of purpose
3. Development of schedule for distribution
4. Fellowship

Figure V-4. Agenda for informal meeting

MINUTES
Flower Distribution Committee
April 13, 1980

The Flower Distribution Committee of United Disciples Church met on April 13, 1980, to organize for the coming church year. Six members were present: Sylvia Bosca, Betty Clark, Mariellen O'Neal, Marion Perkins, Colleen Reep, and Edward Blews. Diane Faw was absent due to illness.

The goal of the committee is to share the altar flowers with shut-ins. This will be accomplished by dividing the Sunday arrangements into two or three small bouquets.

A schedule of arrangers is attached. Mr. Blews will obtain names from the church office each Monday and make the distribution.

A time of fellowship followed the business session.

Colleen Reep, Recorder

Figure V-5. Minutes of informal meeting

BOARD OF TRUSTEES
UNITED DISCIPLES CHURCH
September 4, 1980
AGENDA

1. Call to Order
2. Minutes
3. Reports of officers
4. Reports of standing committees
5. Reports of special committees
6. Unfinished business
7. New business
8. Adjournment

Figure V-6. Agenda for a formal meeting

ncourage all of the groups in your church to prepare
gendas for their meetings.

The second agenda (Figure V-6) illustrates the general
ategories for a formal meeting. An actual agenda would be
nore explicit and could include the names of persons re-
ponsible for each category. The order of business for an
rganization may be set in its bylaws; in the absence of such
provision, the usual order is as shown here.

In the interest of time, it is especially helpful to many
eople if the agenda is distributed prior to the meeting.
his allows time for thought and/or preparation. If you do
istribute the agenda ahead of the meeting, however, al-
vays run extra copies for the meeting. Invariably, someone
orgets to bring the copy!

MINUTES

llustrations of minutes (Figures V-5 and V-7) are also
hown for informal and formal meetings.

In a formal group, of course, there is always a secretary
r clerk who is responsible for taking the minutes.
Likewise, in the informal group, one person should be
sked to serve in this capacity. The function of this person
s to record who attended the meeting, what significant
liscussions were held, and what decisions were made.

Additional suggestions for keeping and preparing min-
tes are:

1. Discussions:
   a. Discussions that have implications for future
      agendas or for ongoing work of the group should
      be recorded as such.
   b. Other discussions of a general nature should not
      be recorded.
2. Details of proceedings that occur prior to actual
   decisions, such as "He said . . ." and "She responded . . ." are not recorded.

3. Names of members of the group should appear in the minutes with their titles and surnames, i.e., *Mr. McKenna* or *Mrs. Albertson*. In informal groups there is a tendency to record first names only; avoid this practice.

4. Accurate minutes can save a great deal of discussion time at subsequent meetings regarding what action occurred. The secretary can assure accuracy by reading back the proposed action to the group at the time.

5. Minutes can be corrected in handwriting with changes inserted and initialed by the secretary. Figure V-7 illustrates such a change.

6. Minutes should correspond to the order of the agenda.

7. The use of sideheadings as shown in Figure V-7 helps the reader to locate specific items quickly.

BOARD OF TRUSTEES
UNITED DISCIPLES CHURCH
MEETING OF SEPTEMBER 4, 1980

Time and Place of Meeting	The regular monthly meeting of the Board of Trustees of United Disciples Church was held on September 4, 1980, in the church Conference Room. The meeting was opened with prayer by Rev. I. M. Goodwill at 7:35 p.m.
Roll Call	There were fourteen members present.
Reading of Minutes	The minutes of the August meeting were approved as read by the secretary.
Treasurer's Report	The treasurer reported a cash balance of 1,782.32. The complete report is attached.
Committee Reports	The Building Committee reported that an initial meeting had been held with the architect. The first plans should be ready by September 30, 1980, for presentation at the next board meeting.

Figure V-7. Portion of minutes of formal meeting

ANNUAL REPORT

The Annual Report to the Congregation is one of those jobs on which you can be "way ahead of the game" by advance planning. You know it must be done; you know the approximate, if not the exact, date on which it is due. Plan your campaign. Some of the following suggested guidelines may have to be adjusted for your particular situation, but the principles involved as advance planning remain the same.

1. Establish two deadlines at least six weeks in advance — one for receiving individual reports and one for completing the Annual Report. Leave yourself ample time between the two dates.
2. Make a list of those persons who will be contributing reports. Notify those persons at least one month in advance. Include any information needed for completing the report.
3. Line up your volunteer staff for the period during which you will be doing the editing, typing, running, collating, and assembling. Delegate these jobs only if your volunteers are experienced. This is not the time to encounter the frustration of working with a very willing, but not very capable, volunteer.
4. Two weeks prior to the deadline, remind each person of the approaching deadline.
5. Prepare one or more folders for receiving reports. Attach a checklist to the inside front cover of the folders for those persons who are submitting reports. Check off each report as it comes in.
6. Two or three days prior to the deadline, call each person whose report is not in. If you have volunteer help, you might ask those persons if they could use some assistance in preparing their reports and offer the same.
7. In the meantime, whenever you have spare time,

begin editing the copy that is in. Make a notation or checkmark on edited copy or place it in another folder marked "Finished." In this way you will not spend unnecessary time later trying to remember which reports you have read.

8. Decide on the format for the report if you are not using the previous one as guide. Keep all reports consistent—typed on the same typewriter and following the same format.

9. Prepare a table of contents, using leaders from the item to the page number.

    Women's Society .... Page 7

10. If possible, run the cover on a different color of paper. In fact, a printed cover need not be all that expensive and greatly enhances the appearance of your report.

11. When the report is completed, lock up the copies in a safe place. No one except the pastor and others he might designate should receive advance copies. Such a practice truly opens a "Pandora's box."

12. Remember to thank each person who contributed a report. This practice can pay big dividends in subsequent years. If several persons contributed reports, it is permissible to duplicate a thank you card and sign it personally.

FINANCIAL STATEMENTS

Financial statements usually follow formats set up in previous years. If your church has such formats and they are readable, use them. If, however, you need to set up your own statements, the following suggestions may be helpful.

1. Before typing anything, check all figures. If you find a discrepancy, contact the person responsible. Do not try to find the error yourself.

2. Numbers are always aligned on the right.

```
  199.40
    9.35
    2.75
7,854.86
```

3. A single ruling (using the underscore key) follows the last item in a column before calculating a total.

```
  199.40
    9.35
    2.75
7,854.86
```

4. A double ruling indicates that the account is balanced.

```
10,354.45
```

5. Totals should be typed to the right so that they are prominent.

```
  199.40
    9.35
    2.75
7,854.86

         8,066.36
```

6. Leave ample space between categories to promote readability.
7. When you are finished typing, check all figures from your typed copy. The easiest way to do this is to run an adding machine tape. Errors can slip by, especially transpositions, if copy is compared to copy.

Finally, financial statements are highly confidential and should be treated as such. Place them in a folder as soon as they are received. If you must leave your typewriter while typing a financial statement, either roll the report back so that it cannot be read, remove it from the typewriter, or lock your office. If you must remove it from your typewriter, do so at the end of a category. This facilitates realignment.

If copies are distributed through an open mailbox system, place these reports in envelopes. Don't invite inspection!

10
MEMBERSHIP RECORDS

Membership records appear to be "the fly in the ointment" for many church secretaries. For some of you, relief has come with the use of a computer system. For many more of you, however, these records must still be maintained in the conventional manner. If you work in a large church with a highly mobile congregation, it is essential that you establish a records system that maximizes accuracy and minimizes maintenance. Or, if you work in a small church where changes are much less frequent, you also need an accurate, simple system.

Such a system is possible for a church of any size through the use of three components:

1. Permanent membership register
2. Working file
3. Family file

These three items, when properly organized, contain all of the information you might need at any given time. While each of these is discussed briefly in Chapter 3, samples and additional suggestions for their use are included here. In addition, a sample line from a computer printout is presented to illustrate how such a system can work.

Figure VI-1. Permanent membership register

Member No.	Member	Code	Date Joined	Code	Date Terminated
101	John J. Martin	3	8-9-80		
102	Mary E. Martin	3	8-9-80		
103	Kelly Kavanaugh	1	9-23-80		
104	Michael Armbruster	2	11-25-80		
105	Priscilla Alden	2	11-25-80	3	9-14-81

POSSIBLE CODES:

Joining
1. Confession of Faith
2. Reaffirmation of Faith
3. Letter of Transfer

Leaving
1. Member Request
2. Official Removal by Board
3. Transfer of Membership
4. Moved from Area
5. Death

PERMANENT MEMBERSHIP REGISTER

This is actually a history of the membership rolls of the church. It is usually kept in a ledger (see Fig. VI-1). Only essential information is included. Since this is a part of the official records of the church, changes should be entered and initialed, never erased or otherwise removed. To insure its accuracy, only you or your designee should make entries into it. Entries should be made on a scheduled basis, weekly or monthly, whichever is more appropriate for your size of congregation.

WORKING FILE

The working file is your "fingertips" file. It is housed in a card or roll-type file on your desk. The major categories are:

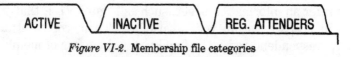

Figure VI-2. Membership file categories

Only essential information for contacting members is included on the card. Since this file should be up to date at all times, changes should be made as soon as the information is received. Some secretaries make initial changes in handwriting and then type new cards when a number of changes have been received. A sample card is shown here.

SMITH, M/M Roy (Karol)

15516 Stonehouse Circle
Livonia 48154

Home: 478-5396
Bus: 476-9400 X400

Figure VI-3. Card from working file

Note that the double space following the name and then the address aids readability. If you wish to include names of member children, these could be typed on the back of the card to avoid a cluttered appearance.

FAMILY* FILE

The major source of detailed information about a family should be contained within the Family File. This file represents a complete history of a family's affiliation with your church.

The file begins with a Membership Application Form (Figure VI-5). An information sheet is then completed for the family upon joining the church. This sheet may be printed on the front of an envelope-type folder. In that case, the information would be handwritten. However, that can be a somewhat expensive supply item, so you may prefer an information sheet, such as Figure VI-4, that you can prepare within your own office. Then, copies of any correspondence with the family over the years of membership are added to the file. Thus, at all times you maintain a profile of a member family and its activities within the church.

Maintenance of the family files can be done on a periodic basis. If all materials to be added to the files are kept in a folder in alphabetical order, it takes only a few minutes one or two times a month to keep the files current.

A COMPUTER SYSTEM

The increased efficiency to be gained from a computerized records system has resulted in their growing popularity in churches. Neither size of church nor price of equipment needs be a deterring factor. In fact, the larger church may have its own computer; other churches may benefit from

---

*"Family" refers to a family unit. This may be a single member, a partial family, or a complete family.

shared time." The range of input media includes handwritten cards, processed at another location, to video display terminals located within the church office. In any situation, the church secretary must make it her business to become knowledgeable about the possibilities technology offers today's offices.

Since any computer installation must be designed specifically for the individual setting, the various factors involved in that decision are not included here. However, a sample printout line and explanations are presented to illustrate what types of information can be available on a fairly simple system.

01-75		WARD PRESBYTERIAN CHURCH				MEMBER LIST			07/08/81	PAGE 1
MEMBER NUMBER	MEMBER NAME	STREET	CITY	STATE	ZIP CODE	PHONE NUMBER	DATE JOINED	GROUP A 12345678	GROUP B 12345678	XXXXAABB 12345678
1326.2	ORLANDO, EVELYN M	15749 ROBINWOOD DR	NORTHVILLE	MI	48167	420-2791	12-06-76	1H0732841	D63122	:1
I	II	III					IV	V	VI	VII

KEY:

I   Membership number
II   Member's name
III   Member's address and telephone number
IV   Date joined
V   Group A: 1   Mailing code
               2-6   Birthdate
               7   Sex
               8   Marital status
VI   Group B: 1-2   Occupation
               3   Membership/baptism
               4   Parish
               5   Small group involvement
               6   Church offices held
               7   Session committee involvement
               8   Miscellaneous involvement
VII   Group C: Optional information, primarily used to record actual service areas or areas of interest

(Reprinted with permission from Ward Presbyterian Church, Livonia, Michigan)

FAMILY INFORMATION SHEET

Name _____   Marital status: Single ____

Address _____   Married ____

_____   Widowed ____

Telephone No. _____   Divorced ____

* * * * *

Business
Address _____   _____
    (husband)   (wife)

Business _____   _____

Tel. No. _____   _____

* * * * *

Date of
Baptism _____   _____
    (husband)   (wife)

Date
Joined
Church _____   _____
    (husband)   (wife)

    Letter of transfer ____   Letter of transfer ____

      From _____   From _____

    Confession of faith ____   Confession of faith ____

    Reaffirmation of faith ____   Reaffirmation of faith ____

* * * * *

CHILDREN	Date of birth	Date of baptism	Date joined church
_____	_____	_____	_____
_____	_____	_____	_____
_____	_____	_____	_____
_____	_____	_____	_____
_____	_____	_____	_____

CHURCH ACTIVITIES

Activity	Dates

(ATTACH ANOTHER SHEET, WHEN NECESSARY)

OFFICES HELD

Office	Dates

* * * * *

Date left church _____ Reason _____

_____

Figure VI-4. Family information sheet

ach person requesting membership should complete this form. How-
ver, only one parent need complete the information regarding chil-
ren.

MEMBERSHIP APPLICATION FORM

ame _____ Telephone No. _____

ddress _____

_____

usiness
ddress _____ Telephone No. _____

_____

irthdate _____ Baptismal date _____

resent church membership _____

Address _____

ave you requested a letter of transfer?   Yes _____ No _____

f "no," do you wish to have us do so?   Yes _____ No _____

HILDREN/Name	Birthdate	Living at home Yes	No
_____	_____	_____	_____
_____	_____	_____	_____
_____	_____	_____	_____
_____	_____	_____	_____
_____	_____	_____	_____
_____	_____	_____	_____

cknowledging Jesus Christ as my personal Savior, I wish to become
member of United Disciples Church.

_____   _____
(Signature)   (Date)

Figure VI-5. Membership application form

Appendix
FREQUENCY CHART
OF TASKS PERFORMED
USING YOUR CHART

(You may wish to photocopy this chart so you will have a clean copy for future use.)

FREQUENCY CHART OF TASKS PERFORMED IN MY OFFICE

DIRECTIONS: Place a mark in the appropriate space each time you perform the listed task. Add to the appropriate section any tasks you perform that are not listed.

PEOPLE TASKS

	Mon	Tues	Wed	Thurs	Fri
1. Greet office visitors					
2. Answer telephone					
3. Supervise other employees					
4. Supervise other volunteers					
5. Attend staff meetings					
6. Meet with pastor					
7. Assume responsibility for meeting specific needs of people					
8. Schedule pastoral appointments					
9.					
10.					
11.					

OFFICE PROCESSES

	Mon	Tues	Wed	Thurs	Fri
1. Typing					
A. Letters					
B. Reports					
C. Sermons					
D. Newsletters					
E. Church directories					
F. News releases					
G. Minutes					
H. Financial statements					
I. Sunday school materials					
J. Youth groups' materials					
K. Vital information certificates					
L. Purchase orders, requisitions, etc.					
M.					
N.					
O.					
2. Finances					
A. Maintenance of contributions records					
B. Maintenance of petty cash fund					
C. Counting of money					
D. Making of bank deposits					
E. Reconciliation of bank statements					
F. Writing of checks					

G. _____

H. _____

I. _____

3. Records management

A. Establishment of new files

B. Maintenance of:
   Membership files

   Pastor's files

   Vital information records

   Attendance records

   _____

   _____

   _____

4. Machine operation

A. Copy machine

B. Spirit duplicator or
   mimeograph

C. Calculating machine

D. Addressing machine

E. Folding machine

F. Postage meter

G. _____

H. _____

5. Miscellaneous duties

A. Maintenance of bulletin
   boards

B. Ordering of supplies

C. Scheduling of church usage

D. Preparation of refreshments
   (for persons other than
   pastor)

E. Maintenance of equipment
   inventory

F.

G.

H.

I.

USING YOUR FREQUENCY CHART

. . . to answer the following questions can help you analyze your typical work week and plan specific areas of improvement.

1. Review your "people tasks." Do people actually require

   . . . as much time as you had thought?
   . . . more time than you had thought?
   . . . less time than you had thought?

   Based on that information, how can you more efficiently work with people?

   MY PLAN _____

   _____

   _____

2. Review your "office processes."
   a. Are any of your tasks unnecessarily fragmented; for example, are you performing a task on several

days of the week when you could more efficiently do it on one day?

Process	Plan for Improvement
_____	_____
_____	_____
_____	_____

b. Are you performing tasks that you could delegate to other persons, either staff or volunteers?

Process	Plan for Improvement
_____	_____
_____	_____
_____	_____

c. Are you scheduling certain tasks for specific days of the week? Are you able to maintain this schedule? If not, why not?

Scheduled Tasks	Plan for Improvement
_____	_____
_____	_____
_____	_____

3. Use your frequency chart to develop an overall picture of your week. What areas do you see that you can improve? Be specific.

Areas Needing Improvement	My Plan
_____	_____
_____	_____
_____	_____

4. Future use of your frequency chart might include the following:
   a. Keep the chart for more than one week. Use a comparison of the results for analyzing your work week.

b. Prepare another frequency chart after a specified period of trying to improve; i.e., thirty or sixty days. Is there a significant difference?
c. Add the approximate time you spend on each task. This in itself is time consuming, but may be necessary if you are to achieve a total picture of your work week.

INDEX

74202